YOU DON'T SAY

YOU DON'T SAY

Random Essays and Fugitive Thoughts

EDWARD M. CIFELLI

YOU DON'T SAY
RANDOM ESSAYS AND FUGITIVE THOUGHTS

iUniverse books may be ordered through booksellers or by contacting:

iUniverse
1663 Liberty Drive
Bloomington, IN 47403
www.iuniverse.com
1-800-Authors (1-800-288-4677)

Because of the dynamic nature of the Internet, any web addresses or links contained in this book may have changed since publication and may no longer be valid. The views expressed in this work are solely those of the author and do not necessarily reflect the views of the publisher, and the publisher hereby disclaims any responsibility for them.

Any people depicted in stock imagery provided by Thinkstock are models, and such images are being used for illustrative purposes only. Certain stock imagery © Thinkstock.

ISBN: 978-1-5320-2202-9 (sc)
ISBN: 978-1-5320-2201-2 (e)

Library of Congress Control Number: 2017908050

Print information available on the last page.

iUniverse rev. date: 08/31/2017

For

Gordon Hammond
Al Rodier
Jim Kozelsky

And in memory of

Paul Weegar

Also by Edward Cifelli

Biographies
John Ciardi
David Humphreys

Autobiography
Random Miracles

Editor
The Selected Letters of John Ciardi
The Collected Poems of John Ciardi

CONTENTS

At Mount St. Helens in the Cascade Mountains in Washington, 31 years after the eruption in 1980 that blew 1,300 feet off the volcano's summit. Photo by Roberta Cifelli, 2011.

PREFACE

You Don't Say is a collection that first appeared as individual blog entries posted between 2011 and 2017 (youdontsaycifelli.blogspot.com). In a sense these twice-told thoughts are a continuation of my 2011 memoir, *Random Miracles*, but this time written in essay form rather than narrative. Often the entries are short spurts, "fugitive thoughts."

In essence these are personal rambles about subjects that have interested me between the ages of 70 and 75. Some of the rambles are based on an oddity I read in a newspaper or magazine; others come from a stray statistic or two. Some are reviews of movies, books, or articles; many are straightforward self-examinations. A few are adapted from my own letters written to editors. Still others are based on science stories covered in the media. Many struggle with a God I thought in *Random Miracles*, might actually exist, but now unfortunately doubt—but can't stop thinking about. All the essays seemed true to me when I wrote them, though I was not so much after Truth itself as the fun of sorting out my thoughts and shaping them into sentences and paragraphs. They are arranged from most recent to oldest.

I left out travel essays, which have been among the most popular on the blog page, because the number of pictures made it impractical for me to include them here. I left out several other blog entries too, either because the subject no longer interested me or because I no longer liked what I had written. I did rewrite and edit as needed—and then went back (most of the time) to update the blog entries too. The result is a collection I hope is entertaining and engaging, quirky and personal, and maybe even at times controversial—which isn't necessarily a bad thing.

Edward Cifelli
Dade City, Florida
April 2017

MOTHER DIVINE PASSES. . . UNDERSTANDING

On Wednesday, March 15, the *New York Times* reported the death of the former Edna Rose Ritchings at age 91. Born in Vancouver, Ritchings traveled to Montreal when she was 15 to join a family of followers of Father Divine, a charismatic preacher who ran a huge empire of believers during the 1930s. She took the name Sweet Angel.

She moved to Father Divine's Philadelphia headquarters of the International Peace Mission Movement to meet Father Divine himself—which she did, becoming his personal stenographer. Father Divine's first wife, Sister Penny, was black and had died, though her death had never been acknowledged by church officials. Sweet Angel was white, blonde, and about a head taller than Father Divine, who nevertheless took Sweet Angel to be his second wife. He maintained, however, that his two wives were one and the same person.

Addressing this tricky issue, Father Divine made the following statement, which ought to be mandatory reading in every writing class everywhere forevermore: "The individual is the personification of that which expresses personification. Therefore he comes to be personally the expression of that which was impersonal, and he is the personal expression of it and the personification of the pre-personification of God almighty!"

It's good he clarified that because I was a little confused at first.

GOD, RITUALS, AND ATHEISTS

The older I get, the less I believe a God—no matter what he, she, or it is called, can exist. It's a pity of course, but there it is. It was always a slippery concept to hold on to, little more than a straw to grasp at when feelings of insignificance overwhelm us—as they always do when, for example, we face death and fear an eternity of not being, at best, eternal punishment at worst. It takes a true Pollyanna to imagine how a perfect Heaven can operate when people bump into their ex-spouses, old bosses, and cheer leaders from high school who still won't give you the time of day. Or what about the evening sky lit by a billion stars in our own Milky Way, which is itself only one of between 100 and 200 billion galaxies in the universe. Now that's insignificance on a grand scale.

It may be even more difficult to believe a creator is responsible for our own planet. What kind of God would put his children in the way of such harm as the tsunami of 2004 in Indonesia that killed about a quarter million men, women, and children—or the 2010 earthquake in Haiti that killed just as many. Some four million lost their lives in the 1931 China floods. Isn't our creator supposed to be all good and all powerful? How could he allow such disasters to his children? Why would he have put us in such a hostile environment? No, believing in a God becomes very difficult indeed—unless he's an evil God, and who wants to believe that?

It may be hardest to believe any God would have created so many beings (in his image!) who are so very evil, like the terrorists who attacked the World Trade Center on 9.11.01, killing some 3,000 people—or an individual like Adolf Hitler, who killed six million of God's own children in concentration camps. How can an all good and all powerful God allow such evil to exist? That is, of course, the age-old conundrum that people of faith, as they are called, have to ignore to sleep at night.

What I do like about believers is that they have created rituals. I am a big believer in rituals because they elevate the dreariness of daily living, give it a glory and purpose and shine. And anything that promotes good behavior, civilizing behavior, is good, whether it's a wedding service, funeral rite, or the singing of the national anthem before a sporting event. Rituals sanctify moments in lives that would be emptier without them.

That said, excesses of the religious spirit promote conversion-furies that cause wars and horrible destruction. And excesses of nationalism have created nations that embark on ethnic cleansing, a bitter anger directed at minorities who are "threatening" somebody's idea of a cherished bloodline and an idealized "way of life." Rituals notwithstanding, we have to fight diligently against the religious impulse that leads to Holy Wars and the patriotic impulse that leads to land-grabbing wars.

Which is one reason atheism is attractive. Atheists behave themselves, promote civilization, stand up for brotherhood, live the good life, pursue answers to universal questions—all without feeling the slightest need to make everyone else think as they do. They are actually more moral than religious people because they do all that without the expectation of a reward for good behavior. Or the fear of punishment. That is: they aren't motivated by heaven or hell. Their belief system is admirable in that sense. Brave. Human and glorious. Good for them.

Now, if they could just come up with a few rituals. . . .

ON THE TRUMP PRESIDENCY, I

kakistocracy [**kak is TOC ra cy**]. Noun: government by the least qualified or most unprincipled citizens. Government by the worst people.

"American democracy is tail-spinning out of control. The election of Donald Trump has transformed our political system into a kakistocracy." Alice Dilfdrew, political correspondent of the JBM News Agency.

"Donald Trump is a buffoon and a clown, a sleazy egomaniac who has left behind nothing over the past fifty years other than a bogus university, a meat-market beauty contest, and a television program where he fired people. And then there's his long and sordid record as a sexual predator. And his desperate hatred of Hispanics and Muslims. And his fear of empowered women. The list of his empty-headed prejudices is long—and frightening. It's a national disgrace that we elected him. We are better than that, better than him. Stand firm in opposition, assert your faith in what makes America great. Be the anti-Trump."

ON THE TRUMP PRESIDENCY, II

December 21, 2016 to April 1, 2017. I expect to spend the rest of my days registering opposition to the Trump presidency—that is, after all, the responsibility of an informed citizenry. But two things have lightened the burden.

First, I confess to enormous curiosity about the national direction now that we have finally elected a true outsider. I might have wished the outsider had been someone else, but I have complained about our cozy two-party system for years, the way party regulars have to toe the line and pick up obligations along the way during every election season—just to get themselves elected. Donald Trump, bad as he is, has given us a presidency that is beholden to no one. At this stage we all have good reason to be fearful of the next four years, but I couldn't be happier that politicians on both sides of the aisle are trembling in their boots. Their own positions are threatened by a man who won't be playing by the rules.

Second, late night talk shows have been spearheading wonderfully funny attacks on Trump, who true to his history, has provided huge and inviting targets. *The New York Times* has made it their prime mission each and every day to expose every lie and every example of unpresidential behavior of The Donald. And as far as I can see, every media outlet is having a similarly good time. So the bad news is that we have to read all about The Donald's uninformed policy gaffes, his unpresidential outbursts, his adolescent behavior, and his embarrassing news conferences, but the good news is that it's fun to watch him self-destruct hour by hour and day by day.

JOE MADDON: A TAMPA POINT OF VIEW

A letter to *Tampa Bay Times* sports columnist Martin Fennelly:

I fully intend to get past this, but here's one last angry flourish. I don't see how any article you write about Maddon doesn't have the word "abandoned" in it. "Betrayed" is good too. I get it: he took the money. We're all supposed to say that's understandable, wish him well, and move on. But if it's understandable, it was never honorable. He was just another journeyman bench coach until the Rays gave him a chance. And he shined. 90 win seasons. Making something of nothing. And we loved him. He was the great equalizer. Within two years after he abandoned us, he has a world championship and we are back in last place. How can you not be angry? How can he not be seen as an ungrateful s-o-b? Sorry to be such a spoil-sport—it's just hard to get past such a selfish act of betrayal.

But I'm working on it. . . .

The back story: After 31 years in the California Angels organization, Joe Maddon was finally given a chance to manage in the big leagues by the Tampa Bay Rays (then called the Devil Rays), where he achieved the success he had always dreamed about, winning the American League pennant in 2008 and going to the World Series, which the Rays lost to the Philadelphia Phillies. He took the Rays to the playoffs in 2010, 2011, and 2013 and was Manager of the Year in 2008 and 2011. He was colorful and endearing as well. The Senior Citizen fan base in Tampa adored him. He was the toast of the town.

Maddon had a strange opt-out clause in his contract in 2014. It was tied to the contract of Rays General Manager Andrew Friedman. If Friedman were ever to take a job with another organization, Maddon's contract specified that he be given a tiny two week window to leave the Rays. (Perhaps such clauses are commonplace, but I suspect they are rare and that this one may even have been unprecedented—and why was it put into Maddon's contract in the first place? Very odd to say the least.) When Friedman left to run baseball operations for the Los Angeles Dodgers, Maddon suddenly found himself a two-week Free Agent Manager, which as far as I know is the only time in Big League history there has ever been such a thing. The Chicago Cubs swept in, dangled millions of dollars, and closed the deal, stealing Maddon from the Rays before the Tampa Bay franchise or Maddon's adoring fan base knew what hit them.

A Major League Baseball investigation concluded it was all on the up and up, that there had been no tampering, even though baseball observers across the country still think the whole affair smells bad.

A Handicapper's Nightmare: The 2016 Election

No matter who wins, we lose.

Hillary Clinton is widely despised across the board. Men and women of a certain age remember her as a pushy, overstepping First Lady with a health-care agenda no one was ready for. There were rumors of high-handedness, which is the most generous way to put it; at worst she was said to throw her weight around the White House. She was entitled and wanted to be co-president—or so people thought.

Then there was the Clintons' Whitewater fiasco, a seemingly endless succession of land purchases, bad loans, and illegal proceedings, according to many reports. Deputy White House counsel Vincent Foster committed suicide, federal investigations began, and various people went to jail. But not Bill or Hillary, who were stained by the scandal but not taken down.

More recently we have seen her as Secretary of State squirming to explain the attacks on the Benghazi embassy that left the Ambassador and his Information Officer dead. And thousands of her official and classified emails were sent on her private account rather than the government's official one. Very messy. Very questionable. Very unpresidential.

And what kind of woman "stands by her man" when he's getting blow jobs in the White House bathrooms? And when the ensuing scandal occupies most of the four years of her husband's second term? She should have kept her own dignity by dumping her philandering husband.

Fact is, nobody likes Hillary. Not much anyway. And many despise her. Who could possibly vote for her?

Well, me for one.

The reason of course is the moronic Donald Trump, the most epic, self-promoting egotist to cross the national stage—maybe ever. He overcame big odds in the Republican primaries because he stumbled onto political gold, the vein of middle-class, racist, anti-immigrant, flag-waving, empty-headed American men—and more than a few women as well. The teenage-tweeting Donald has convinced them all that together they will make America great again—on the backs of black people, Hispanics, Muslims, women, and gays. It has not dawned on his supporters that their inarticulate, loud-mouth candidate is using them by tapping into their insecurities and fears.

While Hillary has left a trail of questionable decisions, The Donald has no public record at all—except for five years on a reality television show, which made him a celebrity in the most celebrity-conscious country in the world. National politics has given his monumental ego what it most wants and needs, for every breath he takes is recorded by the media and the Secret Service are his personal bodyguards. He roars, points his thumbs up, and waves the flag. And he struts around on the biggest of stages, the American presidential sweepstakes. He's an absolute fraud, a scruffy guttersnipe without a shred of dignity. He's such an intellectual lightweight that for years he appeared on late-night talk shows and was laughed off the stage. He's a clown after all, a buffoon.

But through the long campaign season, Trump's shoot-from-the-hip style, his take-no-prisoners rhetoric, his talk-fast-think-later approach to debates and stump speeches has struck a chord with middle-class American men. They've been humiliated by eight years of a black Democrat, and Donald Trump has turned out to be the anti-Obama. That's what American men like about him. The billionaire will make America great again by grabbing presidential power on behalf of the common man. He says he can kill someone and still be elected. He couldn't be a greater embarrassment.

Trump's brand of Americanism isn't new, though. It's called "nativism," and it has emerged sporadically in our history, most notably in the 1840s and 1850s when "native" American white men were threatened by Irish immigrants, who were taking jobs away from "real" Americans and threatening American Protestantism with their report-to-the-pope Catholicism. Nativists came together as the national American Party, which was widely called the Know Nothing Party, and they stood for hatred—of blacks, of immigrants, and of Catholics. Donald Trump, exploiting popular prejudices and widespread fear, is merely the newest Know Nothing. He's an anomaly, a blip on the radar tracking the upward climb of American democracy.

This isn't a case where voters can choose the lesser of two evils. Our candidates are both bad, both seriously flawed. I'm going to hold my nose and vote for Hillary—at least she's a serious leader, while The Donald will never be anything more than a scary clown.

Election Night: Trump wins. The actual numbers are still uncertain and no news source is announcing that Trump has won, but he has. I had it all wrong. I figured the GOP blew the election by putting up the one candidate Hillary Clinton could beat. Turns out the Democrats blew it by putting up the one candidate Trump could beat. But as I said at the outset, no matter who wins, we lose. So brace yourself America and buckle up. We're about to experience some serious turbulence.

Two weeks after the election, November 22: According to *USA Today*, Trump won the electoral college vote, 290-232 (270 are needed to win), but lost the popular vote by some 1.7 million votes. Votes are still being counted, and the newspaper estimates Clinton's lead will continue to grow, though the electoral college vote will not change.

Three and a half weeks after the election, December 2: According to Editor William Falk in *The Week*, Hillary Clinton decided "to virtually ignore 'safe' Wisconsin and Michigan in the final weeks," a bad decision considering that she lost both states "by 0.3 and 1 percent, respectively." Shades of the election of 2000, when Al Gore lost the presidency to George W. Bush because he couldn't win his own state of Tennessee, Bill Clinton's state of Arkansas, or traditionally Democratic West Virginia, any one of which would have given him enough electoral college votes to win the election. Instead, we got Bush Junior—and lived to tell the story. Now we have The Donald—and somehow the country will survive him too.

THE RONETTES, "BE MY BABY"

I play Scrabble deep into most nights, a cut-throat, ongoing match against a computer that chews me up and spits me out with discouraging regularity. But recently I stumbled on a way to be pleasantly distracted by YouTube classical music performances while I scratch my head over seven Scrabble tiles at a time. I like the whole package—distraction, good music, and language. It could hardly get any better.

And then I discovered Ronnie Spector and the Ronettes singing a doo-wop classic, "Be My Baby."

It's a 1963 song with the later-to-be-famous Cher singing backup, Cher's first recording. Veronica Bennett, who had not yet become Ronnie Spector, was the lead singer, with her sister and cousin filling out the trio. The girls and "Be My Baby" were inducted into the Grammy Hall of Fame in 1999 and the Rock and Roll Hall of Fame in 2007. It's still sweet to see them on YouTube swivel-hipping their way into pop music history—and quite a few teenage hearts too. . . . back in 1963.

FRONT-LOADING

I have a good friend whose older brother was my teen idol. He was a gifted athlete—tennis, basketball, golf—and endlessly fascinating to girls who seemingly couldn't wait to go out with him. Which they usually did. And he made money too—lots of it. He had it all. Make no bones about it, I envied him. I'm pretty sure everyone from the old neighborhood did. Of course it was an empty life, even I could see that, but what did it matter? He was having a lot more fun than I was.

Recently I learned that in later life he has not been so fortunate, that he's had a bad time with health, money, and marriages. I was sorry to hear it when my friend told me the story, which he laid out carefully as a cautionary tale. This is what happens to people who are not sufficiently mindful of their early lives, who burn the candle from both ends, who in fact burn themselves out too early.

I mulled it over for a while, then suggested that maybe his brother had simply chosen to front-load his life--that maybe he'd decided to live as fast and brightly as he could while he was still able to enjoy it. Maybe it wouldn't last, but maybe it would. And even if it didn't, he'd still have the past that would forever be his and his alone. "Not even Heaven upon the past has power: / What has been, has been, and I have had my hour." The Roman poet Horace said that in the first century BCE.

I'm not at all like my friend's brother, and yet, oddly, I front-loaded my life too.

My dad, like his father before him, died of colon cancer when he was fifty-five. His death was a relief, for him and for me and my mother—he'd suffered for a decade by then, not just from the cancer but from a serious heart condition as well. Watching him die for so many years, I determined in my early twenties to front-load my life.

Don't put anything off for a later life that may never come. For some, the thought of an early death urges a life of pleasure, but for me it didn't. Instead, I developed an acute sense of urgency to become all I could before the family curse struck me down.

I dreaded the year 1997, when I would turn fifty-five, but I would be ready for it. If it was possible, I would have some achievements by then, something I could be proud of, something my father would have been proud of. My goals were to earn a Ph.D., become a professor, write literary criticism and history, and in short be part of the scholarly dialogue. I earned the Ph.D. in 1976 and have spent the last forty years learning, teaching, and publishing. These are modest accomplishments, I know, but they are mine—the benefits of a front-loaded life.

Meanwhile, medical technology developed a method to detect and remove intestinal polyps that grow into fatal malignancies. Like the death row prisoner who is freed by an eleventh-hour pardon from the governor, I was unexpectedly spared. Still, I sweated out my fifty-fifth year—and am now four months shy of my seventy-fourth birthday. It's a miracle.

Mind you, it wasn't easy to front-load my life with work. I became a classic overachiever—a solid player, a starter maybe, on thin teams, certainly not a Hall of Famer. I acknowledged my limitations from the outset, but I wouldn't let them stand in the way. Work became my mantra. And it required sacrifice—like weekend golf, say, or Sunday brunch. I wouldn't be sidetracked by attractive, long-term do-it-yourself projects and only begrudgingly spent weekend hours mowing the lawn, fixing the leaky toilet, and cleaning out the gutters. I would not allow distractions. Of course, I did what needed to be done at home and at school, but I always returned like a bulldog to the work. Later, when friends and colleagues marveled at what seemed to them an enormous output and asked how I'd done it, I would answer with a question: "What do *you* do on Saturday mornings?"

I'm long past my front-loading days, but even now, by force of habit, I work a little every day on something I call my end-of-life project, a book on poet Henry Wadsworth Longfellow. Back-loading, it turns out, isn't bad either.

THE REVENANT—BACK FROM THE DEAD? OR DEAD IN THE WATER?

It was twenty-six years ago now that a still-young Kevin Costner swooped off the prairie in an epic western to win best picture and best director Oscars for a sloppy sentimental movie called *Dancing with Wolves*. I was barely able to sit through it. However, now that I forced myself to sit through Leonardo diCaprio's performance in Alejandro Inarritu's western, *The Revenant*, which has just won the 2016 best actor, director, and movie Golden Globes, the Costner movie is looking a lot better.

Based on a true story, which doesn't mean it happened at all like the way we see it on screen, diCaprio is mauled by a bear and left to die by his treacherous traveling companions. It's a brutal movie with scalping Indians shooting fur trappers through the neck and eye with arrows—the trappers themselves two steps below human on the evolutionary scale and only the bear doing a credible job as an angry mama protecting her cubs and taking out her frustrations on one of the trappers who wants to skin her alive. It isn't pretty.

The work of director of photography, Emmanuel Lubezki, however, goes beyond pretty to beautiful and should result in the one Oscar that the film has earned. Beyond that, there isn't much to pause over in *The Revenant*. It starts out as a bloody survival story, which has limited appeal in general terms, and turns into a run-of-the-mill revenge story that would turn Dirty Harry into Mr. Clean. And at two and a half hours, it doesn't even have the virtue of being tightly concise.

DiCaprio has an actor's dream in this movie as he can overact to his heart's desire and get away with it just fine. What's more, he didn't even have many lines to learn. And when he does speak, it's in grunts and screams that are mostly indecipherable. My guess is that he'll get his first Oscar for the role, only because the Academy won't be able to vote for it as best picture. Inarritu, who won best director last year for *Birdman*, won't even be considered seriously this year. The Golden Globe buzz is grossly undeserved.

Wolves gave Costner overnight credibility in the film industry and allowed him to make mostly bad movies over the next twenty-five years. *The Revenant*, which means back from the dead, should ironically bury DiCaprio.

Oscars: DiCaprio did win the Best Actor Oscar, and Emmanuel Lubezki did win the Oscar for Best Cinematography. Inarritu unfortunately won for Best Director for the second year in a row, but the Best Picture Oscar went to *Spotlight*, a heavily freighted account of Catholic priests as sexual predators—good theater that blurs the line between artistic film making and responsible journalism. It was illogical to give the Best Director award to one man then decide that the picture he directed wasn't the Best in Show. In this case, though, Academy voters knew in their hearts that *The Revenant* was razor thin and built on tired movie clichés. *Spotlight* reaped an unearned benefit.

$1.4 BILLION

On December 11, 2015, I posted "Your Chance of Dying," which was really about how unlikely it is that anyone will be killed in a terrorist attack, one in 700,000, according to a report in the *Tampa Bay Times*. Today, however, as we await tomorrow's drawing of the Powerball numbers that will be worth an estimated $1.4 billion, the largest lottery payoff in history, the *Times* printed a few more statistics that are fun—and maybe illuminating.

1. Florida has had ten Powerball winners in the last six years, and 207 millionaires in all from Powerball drawings.
2. There really is a curse on lottery winners: 70% of them nationwide blow it all in five years.
3. Last Saturday, January 9, between six and seven o'clock, more than two and a half million tickets were sold.
4. Quoting the *Economist*, the *Times* reported that you have a one in 74 million chance of being hit by an asteroid and a one in 292 million chance of winning the Powerball jackpot. So you are four times more likely to be hit by an asteroid than to be the winner of Wednesday's Powerball jackpot.

And yet, eventually someone will win. Someone will overcome those odds.

For the record: I bought ten tickets on Sunday and my wife bought three more today. That's thirteen chances and three days of fantasy before the billion dollar drawing. Worth every nickel.

FINDING YOURSELF OR CREATING YOURSELF?

The renowned gadfly of American psychiatry, Thomas Szasz, a psychiatrist himself and professor of psychiatry, famously denied the very existence of mental illness in his 1961, *The Myth of Mental Illness*. Szasz, who died in 2012, was wrong about that, and saw his challenge to the profession become little more than a footnote in mental health books, if that. More and more he is valued less and less.

But Szasz is remembered nonetheless for something else he wrote—in a 1973 book called *The Second Sin*: "People often say that this or that person has not yet found himself. But the self is not something one finds, it is something one creates." That one still rings true.

No one knows, of course, what to say when silly adults ask what you want to be when you grow up. I remember my first ambition as a child was to become a garbage man. I wanted to be the guy on the street who threw cans (they were steel then) up to a guy on the truck who emptied it and then tossed the can back down. One of my daughters alternated between wanting to be a truck driver (Peterbilts were her favorites) and the editor of the *New York Times*.

I never did figure out what I wanted to be when I grew up. My career as a college English teacher seemed to happen less by design than by random developments that gradually led me there. But once there, I made two decisions. One was to get a Ph.D. The other was to become a publishing scholar. That seemed to me to sum up what a college English teacher is. Or should be.

So I worked my way slowly toward those goals—and eventually succeeded. But it's the "slowly" and "eventually" parts that I want to emphasize. It was such slow going that in desperation I gave up altogether on the fast track. I simply could not rush the process. I came to realize that inching my way forward on any given day was about all I could hope for—and some days I couldn't even do that. These were valuable lessons, but never during that process was I trying to find myself, but was instead creating myself, in Thomas Szasz's construction.

For me, the key was learning how to take small steps—and learning to be satisfied with them.

ON WRITING BIOGRAPHY

I am an academic. The word has a bad odor—isolated professor-types who live in ivory towers—but I've learned to live with that. How else can a person get his work done? It's a word in my view that should be worn like a badge of honor.

My problem comes from the opposite direction; everyone who teaches in a university is considered an academic, whether he or she has earned it or not, and that is just plain silly, insulting really. Most university teachers never get involved in any serious research and very few ever publish a word. They're frauds. They strut around campus, pompously profess in lecture halls, strike poses wherever they go, and provide the very definition of smugness. And they hate students. Their interest in academic matters is strictly limited to preferred parking and easy teaching schedules that don't tax them beyond two or three classes on Tuesdays and Thursdays. They make me sick.

True academics, however, elevate the profession to the status of a vocation, a noble calling. They dedicate themselves to research and the publication of previously unknown findings—and sharing it all with their students. It has been an honor and privilege for me to be in the company of such men and women—and I feel fortunate to walk a few paces behind them.

I was lucky enough to have two such scholars as mentors, Warren Stanley Walker and Kenneth Silverman. Both men pursued their work as though they were searching for the Holy Grail itself. Walker came first at Texas Tech where he taught me what an honor it was to become part of the scholarly dialogue. It was pure idealism. One didn't publish to keep one's job, but because he was on a quest to advance human knowledge and understanding. There was something positively saintly about Walker's message—and I embraced it. Still do.

A few years later at NYU, Kenneth Silverman taught me about the work itself, the slow, careful, painstaking work. The lessons in patience and thoroughness were difficult, but between 1969 and 1976, I learned, producing finally a doctoral dissertation on the American poet David Humphreys that was published in 1982. But that small triumph was humbling when Silverman won the Pulitzer Prize in biography and the Bancroft Prize in history in 1984 for *The Life and Times of Cotton Mather.* Walker and Silverman were true academics, giants to me, inspirations.

I went on to write a full-dress biography of twentieth-century poet/translator/critic John Ciardi that was published in 1998 and received an award from the influential *Choice* magazine, Academic Book of the Year. After that I tried my hand at autobiography and published my own life in 2011. And these days I am writing a book on Henry Wadsworth Longfellow that combines reliable scholarship with a style designed for a trade readership—popular history. One of my goals in this book is to be so readable that the scholarship behind it will be virtually invisible. It's called "The Rustle of Silk: Longfellow in Love," and at the moment it runs to about 180,000 words, 550 pages. I can almost see the end in sight. Not quite but almost.

Now and then my friends at the 55+ community where my wife and I have lived for the last dozen years in Dade City, Florida, show an interest in the mysterious work that keeps me tied to my writing desk for so many long hours. They like calling me the "professor," but are nevertheless wary of academic types, so how can I tell them about the business of biography? How can I explain my odd academic calling? It's tempting to launch into some thought-out lecture on biography, what it is and how to do it, but that's way out of touch with what they want to know. It's way too much of an answer.

So I came up with an analogy. "It's sort of like working on a million-piece jigsaw puzzle," I say. "You've got all the pieces in front of you (if you've done your research right), but now you have to collect all the pieces and see which ones go where. Eventually you will have the image of your subject, but until you've put the last piece into place, the whole thing is incomplete. It's tricky that way." I'm just like them, after all, as I am just like Walker and Silverman too: we all solve jigsaw puzzles.

YOUR CHANCE OF DYING

Of course, on any absolute scale, your chance of dying is 100%. But that's not what I'm thinking about. No. It's the rash of mass murders over the last couple of years that has given me pause—me and everyone else, if the wild popularity of presidential candidate Donald Trump, the Pied Piper of scared rats, is any gauge. It's terrorists we're all terrified of, if you'll pardon the redundancy. They strike everywhere with recent executions and bombings in Paris and California and Brussels cases in point.[1]

Muslim jihadists are the terrorists we hear most about, but it's good to keep in mind there are also Christian terrorists who open fire at Planned Parenthood clinics, racist terrorists who gun down blacks in churches, and various other berserk nationalists who shoot down foreign airplanes to send a message. For thirty years or more at the end of the twentieth century, the Irish Republican Army waged a bloody reign of terror on the United Kingdom. Add up the fatalities and you have plenty of reason to worry about dying in a terrorist attack.

Or do you?

Recent charts in the *Tampa Bay Times* and the *New York Times* suggest otherwise. Your chance of dying of heart disease or cancer is 1 in 7, a truly sobering statistic that manages not to disturb many people. (Go figure.) Your chance of dying in a car crash is 1 in 112, while your chance of dying in a plane crash is 1 in 8,015.

Guns kill people at the rate of 1 in 358. That's the rate of "assault

---

[1] Paris, Nov. 15, 2015: a series of attacks that killed 130 and left 368 injured; San Bernardino, California, Dec. 2, 2015: 14 killed, 22 seriously injured; Brussels, March 22, 2016: 34 killed, 190 wounded.

by firearm." The rate is 1 in 6,700 for "firearms discharge," the difference apparently being that if you are assaulted by someone with a gun, you're a lot more likely to die than if a gun should mysteriously discharge while you happen to be in the vicinity. And "sugary drinks," according to the *New York Times* on July 7, 2015, kill 184,000 people every year, 25,000 in the United States alone.

It's hard to know where the following truly oddball statistics come from or what they mean. Coconuts, for example, are said to account for 150 deaths a year, champagne corks only 24; ladders cause 355 deaths, vending machines only two—and 450 people die every year falling out of bed.

After that your chances of dying are sky high: 1 in 55,000 for death by stinging insect; 1 in 116,000 for death by dog bite; and 1 in 164,000 for death by lightning strike.

But you are two and a half times more likely to die of a lightning strike than from a terrorist on a shooting spree. The odds against your dying that way are a staggering 1 in 700,000. What this proves is that terrorists aren't nearly as great a threat to you as sugary drinks, which really should carry a warning from the Surgeon General.

"Unprepossessing" and "Prepossessing"

Most of us are unprepossessing. It's a five-syllable word that doesn't enjoy much currency anymore, if it ever did, sort of a bulky word that stumbles coming out of the mouth. Unattractive. Which is good because that's exactly what the word means, unattractive. In spades. Online dictionaries say "unprepossessing" is the same as "unremarkable," "nondescript," "unpresentable," "unpleasant," "unappealing," "unsightly," and "uninviting." Quite a chorus of negatives.

It's opposite is "prepossessing," which enjoys even less currency, though it is a syllable shorter and a positive rather than a negative. No one describes anyone who is pleasant and attractive as "prepossessing." No, the only way we know the word, and clearly very few do, is through its negative. Which makes either or both words even less attractive. Perfect.

All of which is preface to my point: when I look into the mirror, I don't see someone attractive, someone who makes a good first impression, someone who inspires confidence. Not by a long shot. I'm old now, and it hardly matters, but looking back on a lifetime of being unprepossessing, I've lost countless opportunities because of it. It's maddening, of course, but I'm in good company, for most people walking the planet are just as unprepossessing as I am.

That's a lot of unprepossessing people. As of this moment, and you can look it up by going to www.worldometers.info/world-population, there are 7.382 billion people on the planet, and it's growing at the rate of 275 births per minute. We lose only 115 per minute, a net growth of 160 people every single minute of every single day. We'll hit 8 billion in 2024, a mere thirteen years after we hit 7 billion.

And most of them will be just as unprepossessing as we are and will learn, as we have, how to overcome our disadvantage. We work hard, for example, develop fortitude, and learn new skills, both on-the-job and inter-personal. Of course, talent (always attractive if we happen to have any), makes up for a lot of it. But even so, the way to the top is easier for the prepossessing people who can smile their way to the top—an unearned advantage if there ever was one. The masters of the race, damn them, are the talented, determined, prepossessing people of the world, a minuscule minority of our 7.382 billion. The world is their oyster.

But as for the rest of us, I have three words: get over it. Make whatever mark you can on the history of the species—and don't be content until you do. Make a difference. Force yourself not to be satisfied. Work. That's what prepossessing looks like, not the image in your mirror.

"Every day in every way, I'm getting better and better."

That's the self-help mantra coined by French psychologist Emile Coué (1857-1926), the one that caught on in the 1920s, the era of Flappers and Banana Oil. People recited it like the prayer Coué meant it to be—he advocated its ritualized repetition at least twenty times a day, especially in the morning and evening. He wanted the message to seep down into the unconscious mind, which would eventually accept the premise as real. Fake it till you make it.

The "power of positive thinking" is how the minister Norman Vincent Peale (1898-1993) described the same idea, a career-making slogan that he preached and audiences paid to hear—and readers paid to read. It was a good living. And people did buy the idea and tried to keep a positive attitude that would rub off on every aspect of their lives. Visualize good things. Think good thoughts. Improve.

Eighteenth-century Enlightenment philosophers spoke about the "perfectibility of man," the same idea, really, but as it represented a shift to man-centered thinking (and away from seventeenth-century God-centeredness), it became a controversial concept, but one that has always had great appeal. For me at least.

That's what I've always seen, all my life, self-improvement. Growth. Development. Education. Moving past limitations. Becoming better. Every day in every way. Nothing sounds so hollow to me as the familiar line by fatalists that people never change. Not really, they say. "You can't teach an old dog new tricks. You are who you are, and that will never change."

Hogwash.

People are changing all the time, in fundamental ways. They grow in taste, in understanding, in decency, in courage, in knowledge—and more. Every way you can imagine. We aren't destined to make the same mistakes all our lives; we learn from them, aspire to be better, push ahead. Yes indeed, every day in every way, I'm getting better and better.

It's too bad Coué's message was couched in a two-bit cliché—but it's the packaging that's all wrong, not the goal.

HENRY DAVID THOREAU: "POND SCUM"

Rarely are myths exploded with as much unapologetic, joyful fury as Kathryn Schulz displays in a *New Yorker* piece that methodically dismantles Henry David Thoreau, "Pond Scum" (Oct. 16, 2015). In her hands, Thoreau is reduced to a self-righteous, insufferable, antisocial hypocrite. It's a thrill to read.

Thoreau was canonized, Schulz explains, by generations of *Walden* readers who either read *Walden* too selectively, separating out all the well-known passages about living "deliberately" and building "castles in the air," or rhapsodizing over individual passages, like the one on black and red ants. And we also read him when we are young enough to value appealing half-truths. "It is true," she concedes, "that Thoreau was an excellent naturalist and an eloquent and prescient voice for the preservation of wild places." And she also acknowledges his courage as "an outspoken abolitionist" who embraced John Brown's raid on Harper's Ferry.

But that isn't what *Walden* is about. It is, in fact, according to Schulz, "less a cornerstone work of environmental literature than the original cabin porn: a fantasy about rustic life divorced from the reality of living in the woods, and, especially, a fantasy about escaping the entanglements and responsibilities of living among other people."

Thoreau was "self-obsessed," by which Schulz means that he was "narcissistic, fanatical about self-control, adamant that he required nothing beyond himself." *Walden*, she says, displays a "comprehensive arrogance," especially when it came to recommending a spartan "life in the woods," the book's subtitle.

Walden Pond, for one thing, was hardly isolated, with a commuter train line running along one side, picnickers overrunning the place in summer, and ice skaters playing on it in the winter. His family home was a mere twenty-minute walk from his cabin, and he took that walk "several times a week, lured by his mother's cookies or the chance to dine with friends." And when he wasn't walking home, his mother or sisters would bring him his dinner. It was hardly as spartan as he made it out to be.

"Begin with false premises and you risk reaching false conclusions. Begin with falsified premises and you forfeit your authority." *Walden*'s biggest failing, according to Schulz, is that it purports to be about how to live, but it says nothing about living with other people: "Worse than Thoreau's radical self-denial, is his denial of others."

In all, he was sanctimonious, dour, unbearable, and self-absorbed, not so much deep as "fundamentally adolescent."

Amen to that.

FUGITIVE THOUGHTS

Enjoy the process.

Don't be afraid.

Time is not your enemy.

You're only as strong as the last thing you said no to.

The line between giving children just the right amount of healthy self-esteem and stopping short of making them insufferable egotists is razor thin.

"I'm the same weight I was in high school." If that's the best you can say about yourself after thirty years, you've wasted your life in gyms.

There is a disconnect between "winning is everything," which we admire in our sports heroes, and being in life a self-absorbed maniac who has to beat everyone at everything.

Thou shalt not rush. (The little-known eleventh commandment.)

I feel about Columbus the same way I feel about Jesus: I can't believe in either of them anymore, but it's hard to give them up.

"WAIT FOR IT. . . ."

I've noticed over the past several years how often people telling stories pause at the end, just before the punch line, and say "wait for it. . .," as if the wait will be paid off in spades. Which it rarely is. The irony of course is that in real life, no one likes waiting for anything. If you're driving and make someone behind you wait, even for a slight pause, you'll likely be beeped, fingered, and glared at—at best. At worst, you may find yourself right in the middle of full-blown road rage. Patience is not our national strong suit.

Not so long ago, I was in a hurry at the supermarket when an agitated woman got in line behind me. She didn't have much in her cart, so I stepped aside and said that as she seemed to be in a great hurry, why didn't she just go ahead of me? She looked at me strangely, squeezed past me, said thanks, and quizzically asked why I'd done that. I told her that, exercising patience, especially when it was difficult to do, was character building. She raised an eyebrow but seemed to like the idea—and though I can't be sure I was being entirely honest, it was close enough to the truth. A little waiting is good for all of us.

WHEN DOES ONE PLUS ONE NOT EQUAL TWO?

I know I'm not actually schizophrenic or bipolar, but I do have two sides that don't add up. Outwardly, in my relationship with the world-at-large, I try to be amusing and friendly, which too often, I think, gets distorted into a series of compulsively "clever" remarks— or even smart-alecky ones. The impulse comes from some deep drive to make the perfectly-timed and pitched bon mot, but when it fails, it looks and sounds clownish or sometimes churlish. And it's embarrassing. But I do it anyway, because when it works, and it usually does, I like being me.

At the same time, I've spent my entire life being serious. I wasn't always a serious student, though I wanted to be, and gradually did become one. I early on subscribed to the idea that education is a lifelong process, and I've always valued the quotation attributed to Michelangelo toward the end of his long life: "I am still learning." Through the years I've thought as deeply as my mind would allow, managed to write down a great deal of what I thought about, and been fortunate enough to have a fair amount of it published. I've smiled here and there in my writing, but as a matter of principle, I kept humor out. I wouldn't allow it to compromise my seriousness.

Exactly how these two sides coexist within me, I don't know. But they do. And on balance, despite being embarrassed now and then by the failed witticism or the over-serious paragraph, I'm content to be represented in this world by my polar opposites. Consistency is highly overrated.

THREE HUNDRED MILLION GOLF BALLS

In July 2013 I read an article by John McPhee called "The Orange Trapper" in *The New Yorker.* Anything written by John McPhee gets my attention—especially if it's in *The New Yorker,* still one of the meatiest, most literate publications in America.

You can never tell what McPhee will write about, and the unpredictability is part of what makes wandering around with him so much fun. You just never know what's going to get a share of his attention, which then claims a share of yours. He's written famously about Princeton basketball star Bill Bradley long before he became Senator Bill Bradley. He's written about the Jersey pine barrens, cattle rustling, and Alaska—all *New Yorker* pieces that worked themselves into twenty-eight books to date. One of them in 1999, *Annals of the Former World* (on geology), won the Pulitzer Prize for general nonfiction. And he's been teaching a course that has evolved into Creative Nonfiction at Princeton since 1975.

"The Orange Trapper" turned out to be about lost golf balls. The title is actually the name of a ball retriever golfers use to fish their balls out of ponds and lakes—or perhaps to reach balls resting beyond a fence and just sitting there waiting for someone to rescue them. McPhee is 85 now and gave up the game of golf sixty-one years ago, when he was 24, though more recently he began stopping by fences separating golf courses from public roads in order to pick up abandoned balls. Thus his need for an orange trapper.

I am a duffer and play golf just to get out from behind my desk for a few hours a week. Sometimes I surprise myself with well-struck balls and accurate putts, but mostly I just like being on golf courses. I'm happy there, grateful that the game is in my life.

McPhee's essay taught me two things. First, that there is a program called First Tee that has taught the game of golf to more than seven million mostly inner-city kids—who need golf balls. Second, that golfers lose their balls at the rate of three hundred million a year. (At one hole surrounded by water at TPC Sawgrass in Jacksonville, Florida, golfers put nearly three hundred balls a day into the water.) To keep up with the demand, Titleist, the manufacturer of what McPhee calls "the Prada golf ball," makes about a million balls a day.

And so, for the past two years, I've been rescuing golf balls around my home course, Scotland Yards in Dade City, Florida, and giving them to the First Tee kids—about five thousand so far. And counting. Happily, I've already worn out two orange trappers.

THE LONG AND SHORT OF IT

It isn't easy being short in America. Not for a man anyway. The country loves tall men. Women love tall men. "Tall, dark, and handsome." We "look up" to people we admire—and "look down" on people we disapprove of. A singer named Randy Newman had a hit song in 1977 with "Short People" who "got no reason / to live" and "nobody / to love." *The Atlantic* magazine published an article in May 2015 that said four or five inches in height can be worth an increase of up to fifteen percent in salary, which translates into tall people earning hundreds of thousands of dollars more than short people over their work years. No, it isn't easy—and that doesn't even take into account the smug smirks of tall people as they look down and shrug you off as a defective specimen.

And yet there are long and impressive lists of short world leaders through history—Alexander the Great (5-6), Napoleon (5-6), Gandhi (5-3), James Madison (5-4), Josef Stalin (5-6), among many others. The lists of short athletes, musicians, painters, writers, movie stars, and so on are similarly impressive, like Yogi Berra and Floyd Mayweather; Beethoven and Mozart; Picasso and Stravinsky; Martin Scorsese and Tom Cruise; Charlie Chaplin and Harry Houdini. My personal favorites are recent NBA stars Muggsy Bogues (5-3) and Spud Webb (5-6), who barely made it to the waists of seven-foot, two-inch, wide-body centers.

Lists like these, even abbreviated ones like mine, can be impressively long and may suggest that things aren't so bad for short people after all—but short men in America know better. There is a silent, persistent prejudice against us built into our national mindset. It's a discrimination hardwired into our common psyche, into our very hearts, into the language we use every day. Call it a national shortcoming.

POST OBAMA

The nation will have a new president in January 2017, which means the election will be in November 2016, some thirteen months off. The political season these days actually stretches through the whole calendar year, one year after another, or so it seems, with no time off for candidates or voters to catch their breath. It's exhausting for everyone. The more so if you happen to watch television news featuring talking heads screaming at one another. Partisan politics has become a full-contact blood sport.

The energy-sapping futility of it all is suggested by a set of statistics published recently, most notably that five billion dollars is about to be spent to sway ten percent of the voters in a handful of "swing states." That's astounding. Think of all that energy about to be spent. And the frantic spending. And the media feeding-frenzy. It's not going to be pretty—though in all honesty, if you can keep your head, it may be very entertaining.

There are other crazy numbers. As for example that no matter who runs and no matter what platforms they run on, forty-five percent of the people will vote straight Democrat and forty-five percent will vote straight Republican. What's left is the ten percent of undecided voters in the swing states who are up for grabs. And as only little more than fifty percent of the total voting age population actually voted in the last presidential election, all that time and money will be spent on five percent of the voters in the swing states—and they tend to be located in a handful of counties and often along a stretch of interstate connecting major cities, like the I 4 corridor between Tampa and Orlando.

Maybe we should just hold the national presidential election in those swing counties in the eight or nine swing states. None of the rest of us seem to matter. And we wouldn't have to put up with the unfolding political circus over the next full year. And maybe we could use four and a half of the five billion dollars on things that really matter. Fill in the blank with your favorite charity.

ZOROASTER, HEAVEN, AND HELL

I'm no expert on any of these things, but recently I read a book by Harold Bloom called *Omens of Millennium* (New York, 1996) that claimed Zoroaster, the Iranian prophet who may go back as far as 1500 BCE, "invented the resurrection of the dead." Before him, says Bloom, most of the dead passed to an unpleasant underground existence, all except for a few chosen by the gods for something better.

Zoroaster apparently refined this notion by inventing heaven and hell, as we think of them today, with true believers going to the "skies" and unbelievers being punished in an underground after-life. The prophet believed in a "divine fire" that was expected in his own lifetime to change "nature" into "eternity." Thus far, this sounds like the same theological hogwash we're all familiar with.

But I do like how this concludes, for Zoroaster prophesied a savior, Saoshyant, who "will prevail against all evil forces, and who will resurrect the dead." It's hard to know what to make of this, but one thing seems clear enough: the Christian invention of Jesus as the savior who could resurrect the dead wasn't even an original thought.

A NATIONAL DISGRACE

When twenty-one-year-old white supremacist Dylann Roof opened fire at the downtown Emanuel African Methodist Episcopal Church on June 17, 2015, in Charleston, SC, he was, as he confessed after his arrest, trying to incite a race war. He had stashed a handgun in his fanny pack before getting to the church's Wednesday night Bible Study class, and when everyone had his head bowed in prayer, Roof pulled his gun and shot and killed six women and three men, including the pastor. The three oldest victims were 70, 74, and 87, the youngest 26, 41, and 45. As he shot the defenseless Bible Study Christians, Roof said, according to news reports, "You rape our women and you're taking over our country—you have to go!"

Pictures of Roof draped in the Confederate flag and spouting venom from his so-called Manifesto began appearing online and in newspapers. He'd been motivated by George Zimmerman's killing of Trayvon Martin in Sanford, Florida in February 2012. Zimmerman was on patrol for a local Neighborhood Watch group when he spotted Martin, an unarmed black seventeen-year-old walking on a street near the house of his father, who lived in the neighborhood. Zimmerman was acquitted of second-degree murder charges a year later, citing Florida's controversial "stand your ground" defense. Roof took heart: it was open season on blacks.

Roof, however, was wrong. He was convicted of thirty-three federal hate crimes in December 2016, and condemned to death in January 2017. His killings were so heinous that Confederate flags, symbols of the South rising once again, emblems of slavery and the brutal subjugation of blacks, have begun to be removed all over the South, including the statehouse in Columbia, S.C.

Roof's massacre and the ensuing conversations about the Confederate flag have turned the spotlight onto traditional rationalizations of Southerners to absolve themselves of their region's slave-owning sins—like for example, the maliciously twisted logic that led them to maintain that slavery was good for everyone, including the slaves themselves, who were "protected" from birth to grave. Their most pernicious rationalization was the redirection of the argument from human rights to political semantics as they tried to forgive their cruelties by claiming the authority of states' rights. They had the right to buy and sell black people, lash and torture them, kill them, break up their families—practice, in short, inhumanity on the grandest and most despicable scale—all in the name of a slippery right guaranteed them by the Constitution.

To gain the right perspective on slavery and slave owners, read David Reynolds' *John Brown: Abolitionist* (Knopf, 2005). It isn't a perfect book, Reynolds being a typical, over-moralizing baby boomer, but his defense of Brown is nevertheless moving and convincing. It took the violence of the Civil War, and here Reynolds is on strong moral ground, to wash the country clean of slavery, which was always the real issue, not a bloodless, gentlemanly, academic reflection over the fine points of political philosophy.

There should be no place in modern America for romanticized notions of a bygone Southern way of life symbolized by the Confederate flag. That flag is nothing more than a symbol of hatred and barbarity. Every single one should be taken down from public buildings and confined to museums where they can be viewed as the national disgrace they are.

Related story: On Friday, May 19, 2017, under the watch of New Orleans Mayor Mitch Landrieu, the city removed the statue of Confederate General Robert E. Lee from its position in the center of Lee Circle. It was the last of four statues honoring Confederate leaders to be removed, but Lee's position at the head of the gallery of Southern "heroes" makes his removal most significant—and courageous.

Mayor Landrieu, according to the *Tampa Bay Times* (May 24, 2017), "marked the occasion with a blunt speech":

> The Confederacy was on the wrong side of history and humanity. It sought to tear apart our nation and subjugate our fellow Americans to slavery. This is the history we should never forget and one that we should never again put on a pedestal to be revered. As a community, we must recognize the significance of removing New Orleans' Confederate monuments. It is our acknowledgement that now is the time to take stock of, and then move past, a painful part of our history.

"FALLING IN LOVE"

I've always thought "falling in love" an unfortunate expression, especially when it leads to marriage, because "falling" suggests an accident—like someone falling into a hole. I'm tempted to think we should put a little reason into the romantic equation and not let love and marriage be a total accident. (One solution of course is to keep them separate, as in Oscar Wilde's famous quip: "One should always be in love. That is the reason one should never marry.")

But using your head in matters of the heart seems at first blush a huge sacrifice—and it may well be too much to ask. I recently watched a television drama in which an American traveling in Europe was puzzled by a beautiful girl who was engaged to a hard-working, box-like guy who lacked all romantic possibilities. The American asked the beautiful girl why she was engaged to this overly earnest, stolid sort of man, and she replied, "You live in the richest country in the world. You can afford to have emotions." She was using her head, you see. She had made the smart choice. But had she given up too much?

According to online statistics, arranged marriages, which take love out of the equation completely, make up some 55% of marriages worldwide, and the divorce rate is an incredibly low 6%. In America the divorce rate is between 40 and 50%. "Learning" to love is after all different from "falling" in love, but the longer, slower way around may yield firmer and deeper relationships, lifetimes of commitment that are probably very happy in their way.

What a shame it has to come at such a cost.

REPUBLICANS AND EMPERORS

In 49 BCE, at the tail end of the glorious, democratic, six-hundred-year-old Roman Republic, Julius Caesar led his army across the Rubicon River in northeast Italy and thus crossed the point of no return, for he knew his action defied both tradition and law and that he and his army would soon be entering Rome, taking it by force. He knew he was leading a revolution. "The die is cast," he famously said as he crossed the river, understanding full well what he was doing and what it meant, that he was challenging by main force the entrenched, senate-run government that was buckling under the weight of widespread popular unrest.

The very same Romans who were challenging Senate rule, welcomed Caesar as their savior, but overcoming six centuries of entrenched government also created chaos as opposing parties vied with each other for power—which made the government even more unstable. The people looked to Caesar to calm the waters, to restore order, to bring peace back to the city and the Republic. They wanted him to be king, a title Rome had proudly done without for some six centuries. Caesar wisely refused the offer, but then not-so-wisely accepted the same position rephrased as Rome's "Dictator for Life."

Clearly this was a semantic evasion, which led the most conservative Senators, calling themselves the Liberators, to plot and successfully assassinate Caesar on the Ides of March, 44. So the democratic Roman Republic, which had long been run by a conservative ruling class, was threatened by a leftist revolution supporting a dictator who was then assassinated by Senate conspirators. The political landscape of conservative Senators and military revolutionaries shifted so quickly that it was all but impossible to determine which party was actually conserving the glories of the Roman Republic. They probably both thought that's what they were doing.

Gradually, after Augustus, Caesar's adopted son and heir, took the reins of government, the Roman Empire was born and lasted another five hundred years, a long saga of Roman emperors, ranging from the very good like Augustus and Marcus Aurelius to the very bad like Caligula and Nero, a long era of Dictators for Life.

What does this long history of Roman power and grandeur tell us? That the justly celebrated and democratic Roman Republic ran out of steam after about 700 years and was replaced by an autocratic government led by a succession of famous and infamous Roman emperors, all of whom led an undemocratic system that eventually self-destructed too. But altogether, the Republic and the Empire lasted an astounding twelve hundred years. Rome prospered under both forms—then crashed and burned under both forms.

Conclusion: Democratic republics aren't any more successful in the grand scheme of things than the rule of tyrants. Damn it.

HENRY LONGFELLOW AND JOHN WILLIAMS: TYING UP LOOSE ENDS

Yesterday I tied up some loose ends. I had to rewrite a chapter of the book I'm writing on Henry Wadsworth Longfellow, putting in some new information that changed the chapter significantly, and yesterday I finished up a week's work. Nice. Now I can think again about making some forward progress. Lateral is good, and necessary in this case, but forward progress is what I'm after. So tying up that loose end felt very good, especially because the lovely Roberta Louise and I are heading to exotic Istanbul on Sunday, and after a week there, we are going to Malta—the island country south of Sicily and north of Africa in the Mediterranean. I really wanted to get this new information into my chapter before we leave. Some things you just don't want to carry over for even a short, two-week vacation.

Another loose end that got tied up yesterday was finally reading John Williams' *Augustus* (1972). I met Williams once in the early 1990s when I was interviewing people for my biography of poet/translator/scholar John Ciardi. They knew each other from Bread Loaf, once called the grand-daddy of all writers' conferences, where for a few years in the 1960s, Ciardi was the director and Williams was on his fiction faculty.

Williams was then living, dying actually, in Fayetteville, Arkansas, one of God's green places that is home to the state university, and I found myself with a few hours of free time from one of the Ciardi projects I was then involved in, a book that would be published by the university press, *The Selected Letters of John Ciardi* (1992). I was at the same time collecting information for a life of Ciardi, which came out in 1998, so spending an hour with John Williams made a lot of sense.

But I wasn't ready to talk to him, hadn't read any of his books, and barely even knew his reputation. We talked pleasantly for an hour or two, had a drink together, but it was unproductive. Which was my fault. I just didn't have time back then to read some of Williams' work. I figured I'd get to it later. But I never did.

That's how it stood until a man from Sarasota writing Williams' life contacted me for an interview here in Dade City some six months ago. We spent a good afternoon chatting, but still I hadn't read anything by Williams. But now that I'm retired and splitting my time between Longfellow and the golf course, I knew I could fit Williams in. And so I did.

I read *Stoner* (1965) first—and immediately fell under Williams' spell—he's that good. I was doing handstands at being the most recent reader to have discovered this great book. And of course I immediately thought back to that missed opportunity, when I could have asked the man to tell me about the book Morris Dickstein in *The New York Times Book Review* called "a perfect novel."

And then, with all those good vibes about *Stoner* still washing over me, I went online to find a copy of *Augustus*, which won the National Book Award in fiction in 1972. But it took a couple of weeks to arrive, plenty of time for me to get involved in some other book, some other writer, so when it did get delivered to my front porch, I promptly put it aside for a while, until an article in *The New York Review of Books* (August 2014) came out on Williams and Augustus, the men and the book. As it happens, last week I was also contacted by another potential Williams biographer for yet another interview.

The universe was sending me some not-so-subtle messages to tie up this loose end. So I did. Finally, and to my great pleasure, I read *Augustus*.

Neither a small-town college professor in *Stoner*, nor the mighty Caesar Augustus himself can match up against a universe that will have its way with them. That's one of the insistent themes at the heart of both of these great Williams books. But I don't want to talk about the books, don't want to review them or critique them. I was just tying up a loose end—and by doing so discovered a novelist worth reading, worth holding in the highest esteem. Now that's one good loose end. I can leave for Istanbul in peace.

LISTENING TO VOICES

The New York Times Book Review editors asked novelist Dean Koontz what book he thought was most "disappointing, overrated, just not good." I didn't care that he listed Virginia Woolf's *To the Lighthouse* because I never liked it much either. But he also said he stops reading when he realizes the author has embraced his character's "nihilism." I understand the principle, but why stop there? I stop reading when the author embraces his character's religious faith, Marxism, capitalism, feminism, politics, sexual preferences, psychological school of thought—just about any agenda. I don't go to fiction to be instructed in the author's way of looking at the world. I go to fiction to hear a voice telling me about people and places, moods and feelings, the sort of thing we used to call "universal" in our stories and poems. And even then, if I don't like the voice, I'll stop reading pretty quickly. There are simply too many books out there to bother with the voices you don't like listening to.

THE REDEMPTION OF AN OVER-AGED BASEBALL FAN

I'm embarrassed to be a baseball fan.

It would be all right if I were just a casual fan who sees an occasional game, a guy who secretly finds the whole thing boring. It is. I realize that. For one thing, baseball games are way too long. Managers teach their hitters to go "deep in the count," which in baseball lingo means 3 and 2 counts and lots of foul balls. Make the pitcher work. Get his pitch count up and up until the opposing manager has to take him out, which is good because you want to get into the other team's bullpen. That's when our guys might be able to put a couple of runs on the board. Slow the game down. Get those pitchers tired.

Pitchers slow the game down too, especially when they have to work out of trouble. With runners on base, pitchers often go into slow-motion—rub the ball down, walk around the mound, reach for the rosin bag, shake off the catcher's signals, throw over to first to keep the runner close, call the third baseman over for a chat about who should cover a bunt. Lord, a half inning can run half an hour.

But I love every minute of it. It's high drama. And my emotional life hangs in the balance—absolute, pure elation on the one hand, total, heart-breaking depression on the other. And of course, that's why I'm embarrassed to be a baseball fan, especially now that I'm 72. Shouldn't such feelings have passed by now? Gone the way of all youthful passions? But there I am at the TV most nights with the sound turned off so I can read some book or do some lap work. I care. Damn it all to Hell. I care.

Today, however, I feel a little better about all this. My good friend Jim Kozelsky gave me his copy of *Sports Illustrated*, which has an article by Tom Verducci on "The Passion of Roger Angell," one of those magnificent *New Yorker* writers I've been reading for years. If you know baseball at all, you know Angell's essays on the national pastime. I won't heap superfluous praise on one of the great writers of our age, but note please that he is to be enshrined, at age 93, into baseball's Hall of Fame today, July 26, 2014. He'll be receiving the J.G. Taylor Spink Award, the "highest honor given by the Baseball Writers Association of America," according to Verducci. And it's worth saying that Roger Angell is not a member of BBWAA because he isn't a major league beat writer. He's way better than that.

And here's why I'm posting this entry: Roger Angell loves baseball the same way I do—and he too knows that it's embarrassing, but he also sees our redemption. Verducci quotes Angell: "It is foolish and childish, on the face of it, to affiliate ourselves with anything so insignificant and patently contrived and commercially exploitative as a professional sports team, and the amused superiority and icy scorn that the non-fan directs at the sports nut (I know this look—I know it by heart) is understandable and almost unanswerable. Almost. What is left out of this calculation, it seems to me, is the business of caring—caring deeply and passionately, really *caring*—which is a capacity or an emotion that has almost gone out of our lives. And so it seems possible that we have come to a time when it no longer matters so much what the caring is about, how frail or foolish is the object of that concern, as long as the feeling itself can be saved. Naiveté—the infantile and ignoble joy that sends a grown man or woman to dancing and shouting with joy in the middle of the night over the haphazardous flight of a distant ball—seems a small price to pay for such a gift."

I couldn't have said it better myself—of course. Few could. I'm just happy, thrilled even, that this grand old man of baseball has said if for me. Bravo. And thank you.

Thoughts on Joseph Smith's American Crucifixion

Today's *New York Times Book Review* has a review by Benjamin Moser of Alex Beam's book *American Crucifixion: The Murder of Joseph Smith and the Fate of the Mormon Church* (published by something called PublicAffairs and selling for $26.99).

I doubt I'll ever read the book, but I was taken with a few facts I hadn't known about crazy Joseph Smith and the spiritual phenomenon known as Mormonism, which he invented. First, Mormonism is a religion "whose followers believe that the Earth was created somewhere in the neighborhood of the planet Kolob, and that the Garden of Eden was created somewhere in the neighborhood of Kansas City." That sort of thing has made Mormonism such an inviting target for mockery that "there's no sport in scorning it," according to the review—and attacking Smith himself is so easy that it amounts to "a distasteful piling on."

But the reviewer piles on anyway: Smith in the 1820s "began to 'translate' from tablets he kept wrapped in a tablecloth, a series of visions that became the Book of Mormon, a turgid sci-fi novel that nonetheless managed to sway a nucleus of converts." But so many people hated Smith that he was murdered by a lynch mob when he was 38 in 1844.

His "crucifixion" changed everything. Silly and infuriating as Smith may have been in life, in death he was elevated beyond sainthood into godhood itself. He became "a flamboyant frontier L. Ron Hubbard." That is, for his followers Smith was much greater in death than he had ever been in life, for in death he joined all the other "miracle"-making saviors throughout history. And it's also true that by any logical standard, it is no more difficult to believe in him and Mormonism "than it is to believe that Moses parted the Red Sea, or that Muhammad ascended to heaven on a winged horse, or that Jesus was born of a virgin."

Take it all together, and you have a story worth retelling, as Alex Beam has done by taking familiar materials and refashioning them into an irreverent new book. That sort of work gets my attention and applause—which is as far as I'll go in the way of a secular genuflection—to Beam, that is, not Smith. I might even read the damn book.

Follow up: According to a front-page story in the *New York Times* on November 10, 2014, Smith had a "loyal partner" in his "loving spouse Emma," but nevertheless "took as many as 40 wives," including one who was only 14. He even married women already married, sometimes to his friends and followers. Polygamy, in Smith's self-serving theology, was the restoration of a practice "commanded by God" and followed by Abraham and other Old Testament patriarchs—which thus enabled him to claim full biblical immunity for a super-charged sex life. *American Crucifixion* is now officially elevated to "on my nightstand" status. It's time I knew more about Joseph Smith.

WHINING POETS

I'm tired of poets whining about the public not appreciating them. I know more poets than most people do because I've spent my life in colleges and universities which have taken them in as Writers in Residence (comfy positions for poets whose names are sometimes recognized) and as faculty members in creative writing departments around the country. One blogger claimed in 2012 that there were 71 MFA programs (Master of Fine Arts) and another 112 programs where poets can teach Creative Writing majors; the blogger estimated there are at least 800 new MFA's given out every year. I doubt if anyone knows how many are poets. But my guess is too many.

I like poetry and have written about it, and about poets, most of my professional career. But there is no way anyone can keep up with the annual tidal wave of new poets, new books of poetry, and new schools training them. And it should be made clear from the outset that there are many more good poets now than there ever have been before. But because of their sheer numbers, they go unread.

The poets themselves and the Creative Writing programs they come from are their own audiences. They attend each other's readings and pretend there is a place for them someplace else in the literate universe. That is delusional, but it's a fiction they all hold on to—just as they hold on to the idea that they are under-read and under-appreciated. Their usual posture is a sort of hang-dog look of disappointment and lofty superiority, a difficult combination that they manage with the same irritating panache observed in perpetually misunderstood teenagers.

I think maybe they should take a close look at T. S. Eliot and

Wallace Stevens, both of whom worked for a living, Eliot as a banker at first, then in the publishing business, and Stevens in the insurance world. They didn't whine about audiences. They wrote when they could, squeezed it in between other obligations. Nothing hang-dog about them.

GOD AND SUPERSTITION

su·per·sti·tion. noun

1. Excessively credulous belief in and reverence for supernatural beings: "He dismissed the ghost stories as mere superstition."
2. Unfounded belief, credulity, fallacy, delusion.
3. A widely held but unjustified belief in supernatural causation.

Synonyms: myth, belief, old wives' tale.

No one wants to be known as superstitious, so gullible as to believe things that are clearly untrue. We smile with superiority at the person who believes good luck comes from a rabbit's foot, bad luck from a black cat; that toads cause warts and eating fish will make you smart. We're way too smart to believe in things like that.

And yet no one who believes in God thinks he's being superstitious.

CROSSWORD CONNOISSEUR

I'm an old man now and can see that my life has been in a sense one continuous string of enthusiasms that have grabbed my attention and then held on for long periods of time. Like crossword puzzles, for example. I can be diverted for stretches of time by Sudokus and online Scrabble, but only crosswords absorb me so completely that time seems to stand still.

My mother worked them daily before me, and so I did too as a young man, never thinking while I junior-puzzled that I was becoming an addict. I wasn't fully hooked, however, until my wife gave me *The New York Times Ultimate Crossword Omnibus* in 2003, the year it was published. "Omnibus" in this context turned out to be 1001 daily puzzles, Monday through Saturday, that editor Will Shortz pulled out of the pages of the *Times* between 1993 and 1997. These were the first thousand and one puzzles he edited for the *Times*, "the cream of the crop," he wrote in the Introduction, "of the thousands of puzzles submitted to me until then."

Shortz tried to imagine how long it would take a person to go through them all. He thought maybe two weeks of round-the-clock solving would do it, at about twenty minutes per puzzle—and without any breaks for eating, washing, sleeping, or going to the bathroom. My more modest goal was one a day, which I stuck to from September 26, 2003 to August 6, 2006. It took two years, ten months, and six days. It was a crazy-long commitment—and by the end of it, I was indeed an addict.

But not necessarily to the *Times* puzzles, even though they are still the gold standard. The problem is that since 2006, I've been living in central Florida and now have just a weekend newspaper subscription—and I'm not a fan of Shortz's weekend work: Friday and Saturday puzzles are punishingly hard, which compromises whatever wit and charm they may have been aiming for, and Sunday puzzles are bigger than I like. Monday puzzles are too easy. But I do like the Tuesday, Wednesday, and Thursday puzzles, which I usually pick up at the grocery store where I buy the *Times* for $2.50.

I tried the online version for a few months, but didn't get along as well with the keyboard as I do with a pencil—or pen. Using a pen makes the puzzle harder because you have to be very sure before adding words to the grid. The idea is to make the puzzle as hard as you can but still be able to solve it. (I read once that Ben Bradlee, legendary editor of the *Washington Post* from 1968-1991 solved puzzles in his head!) Every solver has a limit as to how hard the puzzle can be, and part of the fun is stretching yourself out as far as you can in pursuit of that perfect difficulty level.

Yesterday's Thursday puzzle constructed by Ed Sessa was typically clever, spinning around the answer to 34A: "1860's novel that is the basis for this puzzle's theme." The answer was *Little Women*. But there were no clues in the puzzle that showed exactly where to find *Little Women* references. It wasn't too hard to figure out that they were buried in the four long answers. 17A asked for the "American Moses," which was Brigham Young, but there weren't enough spaces, so I knew at once that one space needed three letters. It turned out the missing letters were AMY, which provided the pattern for the other *Little Women* references: the missing letters in 10D (Shakespeare play setting: Globe Theater) were BETH; the missing letters in 32D (Ribald humor: dirty jokes) were JO; and the missing letters in 55A (Baby boomers, with "the": me generation) were MEG. And thus the little women were identified and the puzzle was solved. It's the puzzle within a puzzle that makes all the difference.

Here's another typical *Times* Thursday adventure, this one by Keith Talon on July 3, 2008. There are three clues for thirteen-letter answers, each of them with a fiendishly placed error. 20A's clue is "What this answer could use?" which turns out to be PROOFREADINNG. The clue for 37A is "Like this answer's error," which is TYPOGRPAHICAL. And the third clue is "This answer contains one": MISPELLEDWORD. Not only are the answers ingeniously difficult, they are all spelled wrong. Brilliant fun.

Thursday puzzles in the *Times* (and nowadays elsewhere too) are clearly and unarguably the best of the week—especially when they contain a puzzle within a puzzle. And when they do, it's no contest. They are simply the greatest fun to solve. Friday and Saturday puzzles by contrast are no fun at all, merely being hard for the sake of being hard—and it's a given that any constructor and his or her editor can make any puzzle harder than anyone can solve—anyone except the Puzzle Prodigies, who walk the earth like mere mortals until crossword puzzles come out and are solved in less time than it takes most of us to sharpen our pencils. They're a perverse bunch and the less said about them, the better.

It's the Thursday puzzle, then, that packs all the punch, provides more fun per grid than any other all week. Take it from me, a sort of slightly above average solver—and a genuine, if self-styled, crossword connoisseur.

AN ACTRESS, AN AUTHOR, AND AN ENGLISH TEACHER: ADVICE TO YOUNG WRITERS

There's a short article in the new issue of *The Week* (March 7, 2014) about the insecurities of British actress Emily Mortimer, daughter of the late and famous lawyer and author, John Mortimer. She attributes her chronic feelings of self-doubt to the circumstances surrounding her admission to an exclusive private school in London. It seems she was on the "wait list" until her father took the headmistress out to lunch: "I'm sure he told her what an attractive, wonderful woman she was and put his hand on her knee, or something, and then I got in." Making matters worse, "I got him to write all my essays," which was fine, she reported, until the final grades came in. One of her teachers said that her stories were good, "but that they lack that vital spark of imagination"—which made her father so mad that he had to be restrained from taking the matter up with school officials.

The anecdote is amusing of course, and perhaps even true, but Emily Mortimer's teacher does make one wonder about English teachers in general. I spent a lifetime being one, and what I observed was that very few of my colleagues ever wrote a word—and yet felt fully competent to teach writing. It doesn't compute. Would you want to learn about car mechanics from someone who had never worked on one?

My advice to young writers: keep writing and trust your instincts. They're probably a better guide than your teachers.

BEING GODLIKE IN A
GODLESS UNIVERSE

We are *homo sapiens*, "wise men," a species seemingly singled out to walk upright, to speak, to think and reason. We've got a big brainpan. We're special. Made in the image of God, according to some. Godlike.

That doesn't make much sense when we think about how creepy and klutzy we are as humans, how low-down and scheming and self-serving. It doesn't make much sense when we think about how fragile we are in these bodies, how many ways there are for them to break down and die before their time. And even when allotted the full biblical share of "threescore and ten" (not much by modern standards of longevity), eventually the body and mind fail and we are left a pathetic shell of what we once were. All in less than a hundred years. That's Godlike? Surely He could have come up with something better than that, right?

And what about all those bodily functions that are smelly and disgusting? Those are Godlike? And sex. What about that? Heaving and sweaty bodies gasping for breath and clutching each other like animals in heat, explosive orgasms—that's Godlike? No, if the fragile, appetite-driven, animal-like human body is Godlike, we've got to wonder what sort of God He is? Why couldn't He have done any better? What was He thinking? It doesn't add up.

It is argued, of course, that all this "made in God's image" talk shouldn't be taken too literally. After all, we do think and reason, that must be how we are made in God's image. And it is true that we have thought and reasoned our way to greatness throughout the entire catalog of human inquiry. That must surely be Godlike.

We understand, for example, evolution's role in the origin of the species, although that understanding meant we had to give up the Adam and Eve myth. We understand cosmology too, or great chunks of it, including the age of the universe, many of the physical laws that govern it, and even its origin, although this knowledge has come to us at the expense of the creation myth in Genesis. And we also understand quantum mechanics, including the subatomic structures that have explained such mysteries as the formation of matter in the universe, but that unfortunately didn't leave God with anything to create.

So now we have a new mystery. How is it that God gave us reason and intelligence enough to conclude that He has no role in anything—not in the formation of the heavens and the earth, not in the creation of mankind, and not in the basic formation of matter. The only conclusion that makes sense is that there is no God.

Which is strangely consoling. If we are in fact made in God's image, then we have to ask if the evil side of human nature is a mirror image of an evil side of God, which is an unthinkable concept for those who believe He exists. But if God doesn't exist, then everything makes sense again, for we can readily explain evil simply by looking within ourselves, or by accepting horrific natural disasters as the work of an indifferent universe instead of a vengeful God. When nature causes human suffering, it isn't personal.

And if there is no God, we don't have to worry about the Bible either, which is clearly a work of fiction—now bloodthirsty, now lustful—flights of fantasy co-existing with horrible tests of faith. It's a good read, a wonderful romp through the ancient world, violent and grotesque at times, lyrical and gentle at other times. If God doesn't exist, then the Bible can be read as the good book it is, not the Good Book believers cling to in place of reason and common sense.

The glory of the human experience is that we are on a solitary journey through time and space and that we have discovered the truths of the universe all on our own. And while we haven't yet unlocked all the answers to the secrets of the universe, we have probed deeply, asked the right questions, and persisted in our work, and one day *homo sapiens* will figure it all out. In time. All of us should be proud to be part of this problem-solving species that has been walking upright on the planet for only a few thousand years—hardly any time at all when we recall that the universe is about fourteen billion years old. We are remarkable—and we've done it all on our own.

Cheers to the godless. Without you we'd still be stuck interpreting tsunamis, earthquakes, floods, and volcanic eruptions as God's displeasure with His chosen people, wondering just where we went wrong and why we needed to be punished.

Thank God we've grown past all that.

"BUY AMERICAN"

For a couple of generations (and probably longer than that), we have been barraged with frantic reminders to buy American products, to put our people back to work, and not to spend our money on products made overseas. Originally the villain was Japan. We had to avoid the "rice burners" that were putting the American auto industry out of business, stealing jobs from American workers. Hondas and Toyotas, however, were such good products that American consumers bought them in record numbers—and forced Detroit into making better products.

More recently China has taken over as the bogeyman threatening American workers by producing cheaper goods than we can produce, cheaper but inferior, we like to say. China and Third World countries have a monopoly it seems on just about everything we need to buy—and every day or so, I get hysterical e-mails about how we must be ever-vigilant to avoid products "Made in China." Protect American jobs: "Buy American." It's outraged self-righteousness that I hear.

Last week, however, the Dow Jones Industrial Average dropped some 500 points in two days. Analysts attributed the losses to the Chinese stock market, which turned up shaky one day and caused a kind of mini-panic in the American market. So maybe the "Buy American" campaign is finally taking root at the expense of the Chinese manufacturers, ironically causing a dip in the American economy.

Maybe buying American isn't the answer. Maybe the free market that has us buying available goods at lower prices has to be considered right. Maybe buying Chinese actually pumps up the American economy. An odd thought.

FAMILY MATTERS: COUSIN JIMMY

I got a letter yesterday that my cousin Jimmy died. Two months ago. His sister thought she'd write me, but then got busy and forgot, then finally remembered that she ought to tell me. I was grateful for the news, but it was hardly shocking that a 75-year-old man with a history of kidney problems should die of a sudden heart attack. And even if I had heard the news in a timely fashion, it wasn't likely to have caused much of a bump in the flat-line of my life in Florida, a thousand miles from Jimmy and his life. I hadn't seen him in thirty years. And yet I took the news badly.

Jimmy and I are of the same generation, born within a year or two of each other, so his death and mine are one and the same from one point of view. I can't be far behind. And I'm hardly a well-preserved specimen of the species. But that's not why I took the news so badly. Not the whole reason anyway.

Our grandparents, our parents, ourselves, and our children form a genealogical string that connects us. Neither Jimmy nor I knew our Cifelli grandfather, who died about 1931, but we knew our grandmother, who died in about 1950, and we were first cousins of a generation that was born between 1905 or so and died out in the 1990s. That generation of six brothers and sisters was born in America, first-generation Italian Americans, youngsters who made their Old World parents proud by fitting so nicely into the fabric of their adopted country.

Their children included Jimmy and me, the first fully realized Americans in our branch of the Cifelli clan with no ties at all to the Old Country. Our parents rejoiced in their Americanism, spoke less and less Italian as the years went by, changed their diet to include turkey on Thanksgiving, and fought furiously for their new country against the old country in World War II.

They all lived within an hour of each other, which meant my cousins and I were close—and not just geographically. We were together often, especially on the holidays, our parents having huge dinners for the entire extended family and exchanging gifts for the little ones. There were piles of black and white photos in boxes that have been long lost by now, all commemorating the milestones of a big family. We children felt like what we were, the centerpieces of our family evolution.

But of course, by logic and necessity the family slowly began moving away from Newark, New Jersey to the local suburbs, and eventually to other states. We kids grew into parents and grandparents, with our own children and grandchildren taking center stage, a new generation totally unaware of the quirky personalities and the hard-working individuals whose blood runs through them, two and three and four generations back.

That's why I took Jimmy's death so badly. There was none of that old network of aunts and uncles and grandparents to mourn him, no one to call me in Florida at once so I might have joined the chorus of grievers. I find myself mourning today not only Jimmy, but his dead parents, his dead brother, my own dead parents, uncles, aunts, and grandparents. It is nothing less than the death of a genealogical tree that stretched from the mid-19th century to the early years of the 21st. I know there are new children who will push on and live out their hopefully wonderful lives, but they will not be connected to the personal histories that I am one of the very few left to remember. It's silly to be oversensitive about these things—it's our common fate, but still, I hated to lose my cousin Jimmy.

Don Jon, the Porn Industry, and Modern Romance

In September Joseph Gordon-Levitt released his romantic comedy about a young man addicted to porn, *Don Jon*. I know that sounds weird, but yes, it's a rom-com and one website ("Wired") calls it "the perfect date movie."

The film actually has an impressive pedigree, starting with Gordon-Levitt as the writer, director, and star, but featuring as well *Esquire*'s 2013 Sexiest Woman Alive, Scarlett Johansson as the vulgar sex kitten; love interest Julianne Moore as the mature woman young enough for hot sex in the car; and Tony Danza as the low-class New Jersey Italian-American father. Charming. And it gets worse.

The Gordon-Levitt lead character is very much a ladies' man, but he can't get good-enough sex with real women, not even with the Johansson character, so he watches internet porn *after* real sex, so he can have *better* sex with himself. Sweet, eh? It's the stuff of romance in the new millennium. The perfect date movie.

I won't go into the ways in which the movie may actually be better than it sounds (it is), but I will think a little about the size of the porn industry in America, which is the essential bedrock truth that the movie is built on. Porn is becoming the new sexual norm, not a deviant behavior, not something to be hidden away and ashamed of. Jennifer Aniston's television *Friends* watched it. Celebrity sex tapes are a dime a dozen. "Normal" couples routinely record themselves in action. And hotel pay-per-view X-rated movies make more money than mini-bars do.

The actual dollars-and-cents size of the porn industry in America is hard to pin down because of the diversity of the products that have different bookkeeping lines in a variety of different businesses, like movies, books, magazines, adult sex shops, internet websites, telephone sex lines, and more. And that doesn't include the entire hooker industry which is clearly related, but apparently on separate pages in the ledger.

Not all the porn profits (obviously) are reported to the IRS, which of course makes it literally impossible to calculate the overall size of smut, its real business value. And yet in a *New York Times Magazine* article ("Naked Capitalists," 2001) by the estimable Frank Rich, we learn that if all the numbers were added up, the porn industry was earning ten to fourteen billion dollars a year, which even at the low-end $10 billion figure, made it bigger than professional football, basketball, and baseball put together. And that was in 2001.

There are other ways besides dollars and cents to measure porn's popularity, as reported by such websites as CNN, CNBC, and the Huffington Post. As of this writing, it accounts for 30% of all data on the net, for example, with the most popular sites transferring 100 gigabytes of data per second during peak hours. Twelve of every hundred websites are dedicated to porn. At work, 20% of men access porn. Every second, an estimated 30,000 people are watching it, and from a quarter to a third of them are women. It turns out *Don Jon* is right on point: art imitates life.

Update: According to one online source (http://www.highonbrands. com/porn-industyr), porn has grown in 2016 into a $97 billion industry.

PRIVACY: YOURS, MINE, AND MARK ZUCKERBERG'S

The notoriously private Mark Zuckerberg, the boy genius who imagined Facebook into existence, is famous for having observed that the age of privacy is over. In every way imaginable, we sign off on privacy when we post our breakfast menus on his website. And that's fine, Zuckerberg says, it's the way things are in the 21st century. Get used to it. And judging by the wholesale internet intrusions into our lives and the way we shrug it all off, he may be right. We don't seem to care much for privacy any more.

But Zuckerberg sure does. He recently bought four properties around the one he owns and lives in in an exclusive area of Palo Alto, CA for a whopping $30 million, a drop in the bucket to the young man worth a reported $19 billion. All to make sure he keeps his own privacy. He has no plans for the properties and in fact is leasing them back to the former owners, who are now tenants and no longer a threat to the peace and quiet (and privacy) necessary for the good life. Zuckerberg's that is. What's next for the mega compound? Maybe a twelve-foot fence with razor wire. That ought to keep out the undesirables.

The age of privacy is clearly not over for the founder of Facebook, just for us.

KEURIG COFFEE AND THE DECLINE AND FALL OF THE AMERICAN REPUBLIC

"Let's go in the kitchen. I'll put a pot of coffee on and we can talk."

All through my part of the twentieth century words like that were part of my life. When I was a kid, my parents percolated their coffee, the boiling bubbles popping up to the glass top for a few minutes before it was finished brewing. My wife's family used a drip pot that took several cups of boiling water that dripped slowly through the fresh ground coffee beans in the basket below. Later still the electric drip coffee pot took the place of the real thing (like the way electric typewriters replaced the manuals), and I was unhappy about that too, but at least we still went into the kitchen and put a pot of coffee on.

Now, however, we have the Keurig Single Cup Brewing System. My wife and I held out until yesterday, and now the new coffee maker sits on our kitchen counter. It just doesn't have the neighborliness associated with putting a pot of coffee on, damn it all to hell, and I'm dead certain this is yet another step toward the end of civilization as we know it, or at least as I know it. Sad.

I wish our new Keurig coffee didn't taste so good. It ruins all my self-righteousness.

CALENDAR CRAZY

[An earlier version of this essay appeared as an Op-ed piece in the *Daily Record* in Morristown, NJ, January 5, 2001.]

Sometimes I think I need to join a support group for calendar crazy people.

I don't know where or when my concern for the day and month was born, but I do know that I surround myself with constant reminders of moments flying by. My office at home has an electronic date and time keeper on the desk, plus a page-a-day "rip-off" calendar at my second work station—just in case I forget what day it is when I walk five feet to my other desk, which is directly below the large office clock. Of course, the computer keeps me fairly well grounded in the day, date, and time too.

And yet, despite this collection of date reminders, I recently felt the need for another, so for 2001 I added a standup calendar on my main desk at home, so I can now see the entire month, although in my own defense, this one came in the mail from an organization of disabled people who painted the pictures with their feet—how could I throw it out? For Christmas I received a new one, something called a "golf calendar" so I can keep track of each round—my score, my partners, my putts, and my "most memorable happening." (That's what it says, but I've never been able to figure out what it means.)

When I go downstairs, there's another "rip-off" on the kitchen counter plus the all-important wall calendar, where my wife keeps track of all our dinner dates, vacations, and miscellaneous appointments, like when the gas repair person is scheduled to fix the glow bar in our oven.

When I leave the house, I usually carry two calendars—the oversized and bulky one for my briefcase and the slenderer pocket-size one for those occasions that I am without my briefcase.

Perhaps there is some dark psychological issue at stake here and I am in a classic state of denial, but it all seems very healthy to me. I believe that by keeping track of days so carefully, I am controlling their passage. That is, I think that if I live by the day and date (plus a to-do list of course), I slow time down a little. This I know is just an illusion, but it has a good effect, so every Christmas I stock up on calendars, spread them around the landscapes of my life, and even give a bunch to friends and family.

The irony is that with all this interest in time, I'm always late. I have absolutely no interest in getting anywhere "on time."

As the moment to leave for a dinner appointment nears, for example, my wife sits patiently with her coat in her lap as I dawdle. Oh, it doesn't seem like dawdling to me, like trips upstairs to get a handkerchief or my backup eyeglasses or my scarf. What's a man to do? Rush out half dressed?

The truth is I just don't like to rush—which means that to some people I am infuriatingly slow. (That doesn't bother me much either, which seems to exasperate them even more.) I have, in fact, made slowness an art. Sometime I even spout quotations to the rushing hordes, as for example the Roman proverb, "Make haste slowly." And years ago I took to saying "slow is fast," my paradoxical way of rephrasing the familiar "haste makes waste."

Of course, I get my share of quotes back, which paraphrase down in something like respectable language to "get your lazy butt moving." But I just make a note in my calendar to write an essay about it. When I'm good and ready.

COLLECTING QUOTATIONS

On and off for many years now, I've been collecting quotations, like this one from Eleanor Roosevelt I saw recently in a magazine: "You wouldn't worry so much about what others think of you if you realized how seldom they do." Nice. It put me in mind of one by Susan Sontag: "I envy paranoids. They actually think people are paying attention to them."

In no special order, here are others, some serious, some humorous, that I like very much.

"I am glad of a day when I know what I want to do in it." Ralph Waldo Emerson

"To make a goal of comfort or happiness has never appealed to me." Albert Einstein

"Truth is the offspring of silence and meditation." Isaac Newton

"If there is no wind, row." Latin proverb

"I am still learning." Michelangelo

"To live long, it is necessary to live slowly." Cicero

"Consummate politeness is not the right tonic for an emotional collapse." Joseph Conrad, *Victory*

"Nothing contributes so much to tranquilize the mind as a steady purpose." Mary Shelley

"Be ashamed to die until you have won some victory for humanity." Horace Mann

"Everything that slows us down and forces patience, everything that sets us back into the slow cycles of nature, is a help. Gardening is an instrument of grace." May Sarton

"Don't be afraid of missing opportunities. Behind every failure is an opportunity somebody wishes they had missed." Lily Tomlin

"Anyone can carry his burden, however hard, until nightfall. Anyone can do his work, however hard, for one day." Robert Louis Stevenson

"A satisfactory life cannot repeat itself too often." Mark Van Doren

"The art of being wise is the art of knowing what to overlook." William James

"The average man, who does not know what to do with this life, wants another one which shall last forever." Anatole France

"Do what you can, with what you have, where you are." Theodore Roosevelt

"The most radical revolutionary will become a conservative the day after the revolution." Hannah Arendt

"The thought of suicide is a great consolation: with the help of it one has got through many a bad night." Friedrich Nietzsche

"'Be yourself' is about the worst advice you can give to some people." Anonymous

"The difference between genius and stupidity is that genius has its limits." Albert Einstein

Three from Mark Twain. . .

"If you don't read the newspaper you are uninformed, if you do read the newspaper you are misinformed."

"No man's life, liberty, or property is safe while the legislature is in session."

"The only difference between a tax man and a taxidermist is that the taxidermist leaves the skin."

One from Bishop Desmond Tutu. . .

"When the white missionaries came to Africa, they had the Bible and we had the land. They said, 'Let us pray.' We closed our eyes. When we opened them, we had the Bible and they had the land."

Seven from Thomas Edison. . .

"The chief function of the body is to carry the brain around."

"I have not failed. I've just found 10,000 ways that won't work."

"You will have many opportunities in life to keep your mouth shut. You should take advantage of every one of them."

"Everything comes to him who hustles while he waits."

"Show me a thoroughly satisfied man and I will show you a failure."

"To invent you need a good imagination and a pile of junk."

"I pity the man without a purpose in life."

THREE FROM HENRY FORD. . .

"One of the greatest discoveries a man makes is to find he can do what he was afraid he couldn't do."

"Anyone who stops learning is old, whether at twenty or eighty. Anyone who keeps learning stays young."

"It has been my observation that most people get ahead during the time that others waste."

THE GENIUS OF OSCAR WILDE. . .

"I have always been of the opinion that consistency is the last refuge of the unimaginative."

"The only form of fiction in which real characters do not seem out of place is history."

"Prayer must never be answered: if it is, it ceases to be prayer and becomes correspondence."

"Missionaries, my dear! Don't you realize that missionaries are the divinely provided food for destitute and underfed cannibals?

Whenever they are on the brink of starvation, Heaven in its infinite mercy sends them a nice plump missionary."

"Mr. _____ is determined to show that, if he has not got genius, he can at least be dull."

"As a writer, he has mastered everything except language."

"You forget that a thing is not necessarily true because a man dies for it."

"Education is an admirable thing. But it is well to remember that nothing that is worth knowing can be taught."

"Anybody can make history. Only a great man can write it."

"Man is least himself when he talks in his own person. Give him a mask, and he will tell you the truth."

"There is no such thing as a moral or an immoral book. Books are well written, or badly written. That is all."

"Work is the curse of the drinking classes of this country."

"To recommend thrift to the poor is both grotesque and insulting. It is like advising a man who is starving to eat less."

"Nowadays most people die of a sort of creeping common sense, and discover, when it is too late, that the only thing one never regrets are one's mistakes."

"The things one feels absolutely certain about are never true. That is the fatality of Faith."

"One can live for years sometimes without living at all, and then all life comes crowding into one single hour."

"I hate vulgar realism in literature. The man who could call a spade a spade should be compelled to use one."

"One should always be in love. That is the reason one should never marry."

"Men always want to be a woman's first love; women want to be a man's last romance."

"One needs misfortune to live happily."

"I can resist anything but temptation."

"Moderation is fatal. Nothing succeeds like excess."

THE QUOTABLE ROBERT HEINLEIN. . .

"There is no conclusive evidence of life after death—but there is no evidence of any sort against it. Soon enough you will know, so why fret over it?"

"If you don't like yourself, you can't like other people."

"A motion to adjourn is always in order."

"Money is a powerful aphrodisiac. But flowers work almost as well."

"One man's theology is another man's belly laugh."

"Men rarely (if ever) manage to dream up a god superior to themselves. Most gods have the manners and morals of a spoiled child."

"A poet who reads his verse in public may have other nasty habits."

"Democracy is based on the assumption that a million men are wiser than one man. How's that again? I missed something."

"Everything in excess! To enjoy the flavor of life, take big bites. Moderation is for monks."

"The most preposterous notion that H. sapiens has ever dreamed up is that the Lord God of Creation, Shaper and Ruler of all the Universe, wants the saccharine adoration of his creatures, can be swayed by their prayers, and becomes petulant if He does not receive this flattery. Yet this absurd fantasy, without a shred of evidence to bolster it, pays all the expenses of the oldest, largest, and least productive industry in all history, organized religion."

"The second most preposterous notion is that copulation is inherently sinful."

"A woman is not property and husbands who think otherwise are living in a dream world."

"If you happen to be one of the fretful minority who can do creative work, never force an idea; you'll abort it if you do. Be patient and you'll give birth to it when the time is ripe. Learn to wait."

"Never underestimate the power of human stupidity."

"Always yield to temptation; it may not pass your way again."

"A skunk is better company than a person who prides himself on being frank."

"Formal courtesy between husband and wife is even more important than it is between strangers."

One from Drew DiFallice...

"A man's biological imperative is to produce sperm. It's what he does, 24/7, all his life. A woman's biological imperative is to coax it out of him."

Miscellaneous Funny Quotations...

"I've had a perfectly wonderful evening, but this wasn't it." Groucho Marx

"He has Van Gogh's ear for music." Billy Wilder

"Some people see things that are and ask, 'Why?' Some people dream of things that never were and ask, 'Why Not?' Some people have to go to work and don't have time for all that shit." George Carlin

"It would be easier to grow sentimental about motherhood were the prerequisites higher." John Ciardi

"Nobody in football should be called a genius. A genius is a guy like Norman Einstein." NFL QB Joe Theismann

"Marilyn Monroe was good at playing abstract confusion in the same way a midget is good at being short." Critic Clive James

Review of a two-line poem: "Very nice, but there are dull stretches." Comte de Rivarol

"I'm often wrong, but never in doubt." Ivy Baker Priest

"I love mankind—it's people I can't stand." Charles M. Schulz

Review of a bad novel: "This is not a novel to be tossed aside lightly. It should be thrown with great force." Dorothy Parker

"'Whom are you?' said he, for he had been to night school." George Ade

"I've posed nude for a photographer in the manner of Rodin's *Thinker*, but I merely looked constipated." George Bernard Shaw

"Mr. Atlee is a very modest man. But then he has much to be modest about." Winston Churchill

"It was wonderful meeting you. Usually a man would have to go to a bowling alley to meet a woman of your stature." Woody Allen

"Golf is a game invented by the same people who think music comes out of bagpipes." Lee Trevino

"If you can't say something good about someone. . .sit right here by me." Alice Roosevelt Longworth

"If other people are going to talk, conversation becomes impossible." James McNeill Whistler

"No one really listens to anyone else, and if you try it for a while, you'll see why." Mignon McLaughlin

"You must not suppose, because I am a man of letters, that I never tried to earn an honest living." George Bernard Shaw

"I took a speed reading course and read *War and Peace* in twenty minutes. It involves Russia." Woody Allen

Egotist: "A person of low taste, more interested in himself than in me." Ambrose Bierce

"It is inconceivable that the whole Universe was merely created for us who live in this third-rate planet of a third rate sun." Alfred Lord Tennyson

"I prefer the wicked to the foolish. The wicked sometimes rest." Alexander Dumas

"To err is human, to forgive is an impertinence." Anonymous

Abstract Art: "a product of the untalented sold by the unprincipled to the utterly bewildered." Al Capp

"You can get more with a kind word and a gun than you can with a kind word alone." Al Capone

"I have given up reading books. I find it takes my mind off myself." Oscar Levant

Christian: "one who follows the teachings of Christ insofar as they are not inconsistent with a life of sin." Ambrose Bierce

"The classes that wash most are those that work least." G. K. Chesterton

"A democracy is a government in the hands of men of low birth, no property, and vulgar employments." Aristotle

Television: "an invention that permits you to be entertained in your living room by people you wouldn't have in your house." David Frost

"A liberal is a man too broadminded to take his own side in a quarrel." Robert Frost

"England has forty-two religions and only two sauces." Voltaire

"Be careful of reading health books. You might die of a misprint." Mark Twain

"The French aren't much at fighting wars anymore. Despite their reputation for fashion, their women have spindly legs. Their music is sappy. But they do know how to whip up a plate of grub." Mike Royko

"In Italy for thirty years under the Borgias they had warfare, terror, murder, and bloodshed, but they produced Michelangelo, Leonardo da Vinci, and the Renaissance. In Switzerland they had brotherly love; they had five hundred years of democracy and peace, and what did they produce? The cuckoo clock." Orson Welles

"I'm not a snob. Ask anybody. Well, anybody who matters." Simon Lebon

"I am deeply superficial." Ava Gardner

"Humility is something I've always prided myself on." Bernie Kosar, NFL QB

"Health is merely the slowest possible rate at which one can die." Anonymous

"I used to be a heavy gambler. Now I just make mental bets. That's how I lost my mind." Steve Allen

"Religion has actually convinced people that there is an invisible man living in the sky, who sees everything you do and wants you to follow a special list of ten things or he'll send you to a place with fire, smoke, death, and misery forever and ever. But he loves you." George Carlin

"If only God would give me a clear sign. Like making a large deposit in my name at a Swiss bank." Woody Allen

"Give me my golf clubs, fresh air, and a beautiful partner, and you can keep my golf clubs and the fresh air." Jack Benny

"The Dodge-Plymouth dealers have just had their annual raffle, and they've given away a Catholic Church." Lenny Bruce

"TV evangelists are the pro wrestlers of religion." Rick Overton

"If you live to be a hundred, you've got it made. Very few people die past that age." George Burns

"Having sex is like playing bridge. If you don't have a good partner, you better have a good hand." Woody Allen

"Can't we silence those Christian athletes who thank Jesus whenever they win, and never mention His name when they lose? You never hear them say, 'Jesus made me drop the ball.'" George Carlin

"Confidence is what you have before you understand the problem." Woody Allen

"A computer once beat me at chess, but it was no match for me at kickboxing." Emo Philips

"Lawyers believe a man is innocent until proven broke." Robin Hall

"Kill one man and you're a murderer, kill a million and you're a conqueror." Jean Rostand

"Having money doesn't make you happier. I have fifty million dollars, but I'm just as happy as when I had forty-eight." Arnold Schwarzenegger

"We are here on earth to do good unto others. What the others are here for, I have no idea." W. H. Auden

HARD TO BELIEVE

I just returned from a memorial service for a friend who died last week. I expected the now-normal "celebration" of the dead person's life, with pictures of her at every age and hair style, favorite songs playing in the background, and images of loving grandchildren with their gramma all pinned artistically on the walls. It's usually an unbearable display of unredeemed sentimentality, but it's the sort of thing one has to put up with these days without even looking sour and disapproving. I can do that.

Today, instead of the expected celebration, the churchful of friends and relatives got an old-fashioned mass for the dead, that plus a special speaker, whose name and relationship to the dead woman I couldn't quite catch, and who took too long to say nice things that dissolved into mumbles by the time they reached those of us in the back rows. If anything, it was more unbearable even than the dreaded celebration.

My own relationship with God has flourished and floundered intermittently through most of my life, but in recent years it has deteriorated badly—and now has disappeared completely. Earlier this century, when I was writing an autobiography, *Random Miracles* (2011), I thought perhaps God might exist as the match that set the Big Bang in motion. And once one admits to the possibility of a God, it becomes possible to think of Him as an entity a man ought to thank for whatever good has crept into his life. Wishful thinking, I think now. These days about the best I can hope for is the possibility of a Creator who may have had a hand in the origins of the universe but who lost interest almost immediately, dropped out, and is currently unavailable. We're totally on our own.

Everyone more or less knows this. Where exactly is God in the large universe we live in or in the small genetic one that lives within us? As questions about the formation of the universe, the creation of matter, evolutionary biology, and the operation of quantum mechanics have all been partly answered by scientists who are pursuing the remaining questions with single-minded devotion, there is no further need for supernaturalism and superstition, no need for God as an explanation for what we couldn't previously understand.

Religious folks, however, can't or won't give up the other-worldly superstructure they've become accustomed to—God, heaven, hell, the Bible, Adam and Eve, the whole thing. They say they still believe in all that, although it is probably just that they can't face death without the promise of life after death. Jesus and the Resurrection. Religious folks think of themselves as rational beings in everything else, of course, but in this one case they are completely blind to science and proudly proclaim their "blind faith." And then to draw further attention to their abandonment of rationality, the proudly pious assume an air of sanctimonious superiority. It's an unattractive defensive posture—but it's totally understandable. I wish I could be one of them.

DAN BROWN'S *INFERNO—* FIRST THOUGHTS

Dan Brown is back on his game with his new novel *Inferno,* which puts the failure of his (nevertheless best-selling) last novel, *The Lost Symbol,* behind him once and for all. It's good news for Brown, of course, but it's also good news for the millions of readers who have been hoping to see more of the high octane writing they loved so much in *The Da Vinci Code.*

Of course, Brown has his critics, readers who object to discursive novels that are part travel books, part art history lessons, part symbol chases, and only part mystery and suspense. For me, however, and for millions of others if we can trust Brown's sales figures, the balance of these parts is effortless fun, popular fiction with an engaging intellectual twist.

But the new book will surely drive Brown's critics just a little crazier than the earlier books did because it adds yet another level of talk, this time on the evils of eugenics and overpopulation. *Inferno* focuses on the planet's inability to supply the needs of an increasing population that, at its current rate of growth, will one day soon become bigger than the ecosystems that have so far sustained it. Figuring out the moral rights and wrongs facing the characters (and all the rest of us) is half the fun of the book, and the other half is realizing that easy conclusions are impossible, that the issues are more complicated than they at first appear to be.

The moral consequences of the story, however, are woven neatly into the narrative, which is typically convoluted in the Brown fashion, full of twists and turns that pivot on symbols and hidden messages in art works and buildings. Robert Langdon, the art historian professor-hero of four Brown novels now, is so super-humanly tuned into the art and architecture of *Inferno* that Brown sheepishly defends his hero by explaining that he has an "eidetic" memory, which is one "marked by extraordinarily detailed and vivid recall of visual images," according to one online definition. It's not necessary for us to know this, but it doesn't hurt either. Langdon is clearly better able to connect the dots of history and art and architecture than anyone who ever lived, but, okay, I can live with that. It puts the fun in motion.

The literary and architectural images in Brown's *Inferno* are from Dante's *Inferno* as well as Dante's city, Florence, where half the novel takes place before heading up to Venice for another large chunk of narrative. Langdon must solve more than one mystery at a time in this book, however, which takes him from one museum to another, one religious or public building to another, one painter and painting to another, and finally one country to another, for the last quarter of the book takes place in Istanbul, where East meets West. The new book is no *Da Vinci Code*, but it's Dan Brown at a high level. Good reading.

In the end, readers either love the wild ride of Robert Langdon and thrill to the social and moral implications of the story—or like British critic Jake Kerridge in the *Daily Telegraph*, hate Brown and his new book. "As a stylist, Brown gets better and better," Kerridge writes, "where he once was abysmal, he is now just very poor." Happy phrasing, but too harsh. Apparently popularity like Brown's needs to be attacked by self-styled arbiters of taste, like Kerridge, who feels personally wounded that Brown has found a voice and a character and a formula that readers in huge numbers like reading. He probably hates Dickens too.

Sales note: *Inferno* was the best-selling book of 2013, according to *USA Today*, the third year Brown has topped the list. The others were 2004 and 2006, both for *The Da Vinci Code*.

A DECADE OF
THE DA VINCI CODE

The Da Vinci Code by Dan Brown is celebrating its Tenth Anniversary this month and has sold, according to its publisher in a recent *New York Times* ad, an astonishing 81 million copies. It dominated the *Times* best seller list for 136 straight weeks—more than two and a half years. The *USA Today* reported that it led the best seller list for two different years, 2004 (after initial publication) and 2006 (after its rerelease when the movie appeared). The publisher claimed after its first year of sales that the book sold more copies in a single year than any other adult novel, ever. I was there at the outset in the spring 2003, first buying a copy and falling immediately under its spell, and then later buying the audio version that I listened to in the car. I couldn't get enough of it.

Eighty-one million's a lot, but there are a few adult novels that have done better, like Charles Dickens' *A Tale of Two Cities* (1859), which has sold a nearly incomprehensible 200 million copies in 153 years, undoubtedly a figure that has been dramatically inflated because the public-domain book has gone through uncountable editions and been force-fed to endless numbers of bored high school students. J. R. R. Tolkien's *The Lord of the Rings* (1954-55) has sold a slightly less astonishing 150 million (in 57 years). Agatha Christie's 1939 *And Then There Were None* sold 100 million. J. D. Salinger's 1951 *The Catcher in the Rye* trails *The Da Vinci Code* by 20 million and Vladimir Nabokov's 1955 *Lolita* trails it by 30 million. So 81 million copies in a decade is impressive by any standard, especially when you add in the number of other readers who got the book from libraries, audio editions, eBooks, online and brick-and-mortar used book markets, and the uncountable number of personal copies that were (and still are) being passed around among family and friends.

Like so many others, I read all Brown's earlier books too. They were mostly a waste of time, although *Angels and Demons* (2000) introduced protagonist Robert Langdon to us and promised something better to come, which of course happened three years later with the phenomenon of *The Da Vinci Code*. In 2009 a third book in the Langdon series was published, *The Lost Symbol*, but it was a terrible disappointment for everyone hoping for another *Da Vinci Code*. The Freemasons were not as much fun as conspiratorial antagonists as the Catholic Church had been. Brown's fans, myself included, are hoping for a return to form in his new book, *Inferno*, which is scheduled for publication next month, but realistically, the chances are slim to zero that he will capture lightning in a bottle again. For now, however, hopes are running high.

With all the prepublication hoopla attending to the birth of this new book, I had to pick up *The Da Vinci Code* once again, maybe one last time, just to see how much I still might enjoy it. And perhaps in one sense it is a surprise that I still like it very much. I remember a lunch I had in 2005 with my daughter Laura, then an editor at New American Library, and another editor at the same firm, Tracy Bernstein, in charge of Signet Classics, which published introductions, prefaces, and afterwords of mine for books by Dante, Milton, and Longfellow. My daughter and my editor seemed pleased with themselves when, between soup and salad, they ambushed me about my feelings on *The Da Vinci Code*. Why, they seemed to be saying with mischievous grins, does a man with a taste for the classics, like Dan Brown's potboiler and Super Best Seller?

I didn't take the bait, squirmed a little bit, and then repeated what an old friend once told me about his main criterion for judging books. He said he liked the ones he finished. That was glib and evasive and maybe partly true, but I really did want to say something more serious and thoughtful about the book that had, after all, captured my imagination as no other popular novel ever had before. If I *had* taken the bait, I might have said something like this.

First, the book is fun to read from first page to last, a fast-paced murder mystery with attractive lead characters. Second, there are several very evil villains who take turns with the attention of the good guys and all the readers too. But overlaid onto the murder mystery grid is an entire structure of religious conspiracy so persuasive as to make us wonder what part of the construction is true—or if all of it is. Or none.

Then there is the code itself, the hidden messages said to have been left by Leonardo Da Vinci in his masterworks. We are told by Brown that Da Vinci was a member of a secret society called the "Priory of the Scion," whose mission was to preserve the truth that Jesus was secretly married to Mary Magdalene, the heart of the "sacred feminine" and the mother of Jesus' children. It is all very plausible, so plausible in fact, that it has spawned a cottage industry of Christian scholars forced to find exactly where Brown went wrong with his facts. All of which is amusing: this is a novel, after all, a piece of fiction, so one doesn't demand of it the same standard of truth that non-fiction has to meet. For all I know, there may be some truth to it, but it has been fun watching the Christian world take to battle stations just to "prove" that Brown was wrong about Jesus and Mary.

I am not a huge fan of pop fiction, not even the escapist enticements of murder mysteries, but this is a mystery novel about a conspiracy supposedly hiding big secrets in the Catholic Church. It contains a stunningly tempting argument. Then there is the Holy Grail and "sacred feminine" to bring into the conversation. What fun! I can't understand why everyone in the country hasn't bought a copy. Or at least borrowed a friend's—or taken one out of the library.

I wish I might have said something like that at the soup and salad lunch with my daughter and my editor, but I do feel a little easier now that I got around to saying it here. Finally.

RUTH ANN AND A
LIFETIME OF TEACHING

Three months ago I heard from a student I taught thirty years ago, Ruth Ann Peters, who sits today at the very edges of my memory, her features blurry after a lifetime of classes and students. Dredging faces up from the muddy past is asking too much of a memory that weakens rather than sharpens as the years roll by. That's the curse of a long career in the classroom. But Ruth Ann is different, for even though I no longer have a firm memory of her features, I do have a firm and warm sense that we had a good connection all those many years ago, that we in fact liked each other. That, of course, is not unusual, for over the years there were many to like—it's the best part of the job, even if the individual images fade slowly into the dim past.

Ruth Ann saw I was registered on Facebook and sent me a note late in December 2012, hoping to "reconnect." I replied politely of course, and then she wrote something back that I will always treasure: "My favorite Cifelli memory," she wrote, "is that you once gave me an A- on a paper and a comment that read, 'This grade has more to do with your intelligence than your diligence.' It has stuck with me till today reminding me that good is not good enough if I know I can do better!" Imagine that a single seed sewn three decades ago rooted itself and still thrives in the life of a student I barely remember these many years later. I couldn't be more thrilled.

Teachers realize early on that happy classroom memories generally dissolve into cool, thin air as the years march along. Holding onto them is as difficult as grabbing mercury—and then

Miss Ruth Ann suddenly appears with a wonderful moment from 1983, a moment guaranteed to warm a January day thirty years later. What a wonderful surprise. And to Ruth Ann, thank you my dear, it means a lot.

Adapted from a Letter to the Editor of the *Tampa Bay Times*, February 18, 2013.

THE POPE'S RESIGNATION MYSTERY

Here's what seems odd about Pope Benedict XVI's resignation: Every really old pope over the past 600 years, since the last resignation, has probably grown too intellectually and physically feeble to do the job well. It's a lifetime position, and often lifetimes drag on beyond the point when anyone can do a good job. Which leads to the conclusion that over the last 600 years deputies have from time to time stepped in quietly to continue the work until the doddering old pope finally dies.

So what makes this pope's condition different from any of the other old popes before him? Why aren't there papal helpers who can step in under the radar and take care of business for his last few years? Or is he being pushed out under the weight of pedophile priest and Vatican bank scandals? That's an unpleasant thought, but it makes more sense than that no Vatican staffers could be found to step up and silently help the pope through his last faltering months and years.

FABIOLA GIANOTTI, PERSON OF THE YEAR

Time magazine (Dec. 31) has named Fabiola Gianotti one of its five Persons of the Year for her work in discovering the Higgs boson at the European Organization for Nuclear Research (CERN). This is the boson that has been called the "God particle" because it explains the origin of matter in the universe. Gianotti and her physicist colleague, Joe Incandela, have, as *Time* puts it, "nailed the particle that gives other fundamental particles their mass."

Apparently proof of the Higgs boson's existence is quite a relief for several reasons. First, basic particles do not necessarily have mass; the photon, for example, which is the basic quantum of light, has no mass. So physicists can breathe easier now that they have confirmed in the lab what they (and everyone else) can see quite clearly but hadn't been able to exactly explain until now. Mass exists—and now we know why—or rather how—matter was and is created.

Physicists are relieved too because now they don't have to explain the absence of mass. That condition would have been hard to square with what we can see in the real world. If there had been a universe without mass, quantum mechanics would have been forced to explain how something (a universe) could be made of nothing (particles without mass). That's a tough one.

Finally, the Higgs boson has provided the last piece of the puzzle known as the "standard model," which is an even trickier concept than the business of creating mass. *Time* puts it this way: "The so-called standard model of physics, [is] the grand framework that ties together the universe's three great forces—the strong force, the weak force and electromagnetism—and governs the behavior of sub-atomic particles." By confirming the standard model, the Higgs boson has shown that the last fifty years spent looking for it have not been a stroll down a dead end street.

Persons of the year aside, it's absolutely breathtaking to contemplate everything that is going on within every atom every minute of every day, stretching back in time to the origin of the universe some 13.5 billion years ago. It's astonishing that sub-atomic particles even have an observable "behavior." And we have Fabiola Gianotti (and Joe Incandela) to thank for proving the Higgs boson actually does exist, thereby showing not only how particles get their mass, but also confirming one of the predictions of the so-called "standard model." Everything is now locked neatly into place.

Unless or until, that is, Ms. Gianotti looks even deeper into atoms to discover new facts that create new mysteries that will launch the next generation of quantum mechanics in a new direction that will take another century or so to examine and re-examine before a new theory emerges that will in turn launch new investigations with new problems to resolve. Which the next generation after them will address. It's the way of science, the way of the world, the way of *homo sapiens*: rational man. We probe, dig deeper, ask a never-ending series of questions. This is humankind at its very best.

EVERYTHING CHANGES, EXCEPT. . .

One of the boring truisms observed by everyone at one point or another is that everything changes. The only thing you can be certain of is that nothing stays the same. When the thought first hits us, we feel we've struck upon one of the great liberating truths of the ages, but we soon figure out that all we have stumbled upon is another cliché. Today is the first day of the rest of your life.

When you look at the number of variables that go into any presidential election, for example, like the one just past where Pres. Barack Obama ran against former Massachusetts governor Mitt Romney, you might recall the unknown quantities: the Christian right vote; the black vote, the women vote, the Latino vote, the white male vote, the young vote, the old vote, the Mormon vote, and probably a dozen others.

Then there were the issues: the economy, the wars, Obamacare, Medicare, Medicaid, taxes, the real estate collapse, the loss of jobs to China and other countries. Who was "right" or "righter" and how often? The entire mix of variables that make up the present and that will combine into an unpredictable future that will in turn become a future present (and so on dizzyingly ad infinitum)—all somehow sort themselves out through time, and, in this case, on November 6, 2012, Pres. Obama handily defeated Gov. Romney.

And suddenly, just like that, the shimmering, never-certain future becomes part of the solid, never-changing past. What's more, the constancy of history is a blessed relief after long and tiresome question marks about the future. One of the ways this has been expressed, the best way in my reading, was by the Roman poet Horace (first-century BCE), who wrote "Happy the Man":

> Happy he, and happy he alone,
> is the man who can call today his own,
> the man who, secure within, can say:
> Tomorrow do thy worst, for I have lived today.
>
> Whether fair or foul or rain or shine,
> all my days, in spite of fate, are mine.
> Not even Heaven upon the past has power:
> What has been, has been, and I have had my hour.

Those last two lines are magnificent, proud and humble and brave all at the same time: "I have had my hour." Nothing will ever change that—or the implied obligation to use each new one wisely.

SYMMETRY

I like order. Not excessively or all the time, but on balance, I like to see orderliness whenever it shows itself. I admire form. I am pleased by the firmness of structure.

Now, having said that, I must also say that there isn't as much of that firm structure in my life to suit me. I tend to be excessive about most things, never moderate or balanced. I notice order in my life more by its absence than its presence.

And then, to annoy me further, there is Werner Heisenberg's 1927 "uncertainty principle," which has taught us that order is an illusion, both in quantum mechanics and cosmology, the largest and smallest of scientific investigations. Whatever order we once thought we observed in nature and hoped to duplicate in our lives is, in cold brutal fact, little more than wishful thinking.

Which is one reason we like art and music and poetry so much. Poetry, Robert Frost once remarked, is a "momentary stay against confusion." That's what we like about it. It imposes order on chaos. For the time you spend in a Robert Frost poem (though clearly not in all poems) you can look forward to the blessed relief of a sturdy substructure holding the whole thing up. No wonder he and all the formalists will never go out of style; they're like classic tweeds or pearls with a black dress. Elegant.

All this old-fashioned, formalist thinking came to mind on page 49 of the September 2012 issue of the *Smithsonian Magazine*, where there is a poem by Amit Majmudar called, "Pattern and Snarl." It's an Italian sonnet (invented by Petrarch 800 years ago), one of the most rock-ribbed (not to say rigid) of poetic forms, and one that the New Formalists love to spin out just to prove that old forms can fit nicely with new realities, if you want them to, and if you're poet enough to pull it off.

Majmudar's sonnet is not about a person or about love or about death, but it's about the idea of orderliness itself. The opening eight lines set up the problem: "Life likes a little mess. All patterns need a snarl." He thinks about that idea for the opening eight lines that set things up, and then he resolves the problem in the six-line conclusion:

> What *is* it about order that we love? This sense,
>   Maybe, that a secret informs the pattern?
>
> Is it a toddler's joy in doing things again?
> Is it the entropy in us that warms to pattern?
>
> I never intended this line to rhyme on *again* again.
> Then again sometimes it's the snarl that adorns the pattern.

The joy of this poem is in its reminder that life likes a "little mess," a "snarl that adorns the pattern," which all by itself is an insight worth having, but Majmudar delivers it in a tight pattern that is itself slightly snarled, thus duplicating the message in the form, which raises the achievement tenfold. The poem explodes into a gorgeous but miniature fireworks display.

In the end, we get an irresistible poem about the dual realities of loving patterns and living with snarls. My problem exactly.

SPIELBERG, DAY-LEWIS, AND *LINCOLN*: MY (RE)VIEW

Steven Spielberg's just-opened treatment of the Lincoln myth stars Daniel Day-Lewis. Both director and star are given to excess, so it may come as a surprise that this marriage is not a strained struggle of over-sized egos. Instead, *Lincoln* is an important film that covers the political maneuverings that led to the passage of the 13th Amendment outlawing slavery and takes place in about a thirty-day period in early 1865. More, it is an eerily photographic treatment that seems taken out of the pages of Civil War photojournalism. But it is not a good movie.

The chief reason for this is its unrelenting barrage of talk. Tony Kushner's first version of the screenplay ran to an unheard-of 500 pages, which he whittled down to about 130 pages that unreel in two and a half hours. The length would not have been a problem had it not been for a serious imbalance between talk and action: there isn't much motion in this motion picture.

Making matters worse for the audience is that the characters, although based on real people, are mostly unknown today. We do not automatically know what their political positions were, what the congressional alliances looked like, or even why all the Northerners did not have similar thoughts about a constitutional amendment to outlaw slavery. Nor are we in on the political dialogue or even the vocabulary of the time; the very words "Republican" and "Democrat," and the parties they represent, are roughly opposite to their modern counterparts.

Lincoln's own political and moral positions are also hard to pin down because the film doesn't show how he had morphed from a

Colonizationist (in favor of relocating slaves back to Africa) to the author of the Emancipation Proclamation and the engineer of the 13th Amendment.

Not all of Kushner's words are political, however. Just to break things up, there are occasional passages between Mr. and Mrs. Lincoln in marital strife—words about her madness, their dead son Willy, and their relationship. The Abraham vs. Mary drama is loud, but not character-revealing. One would have to go into the movie theater with knowledge of Mary Lincoln's fragile mental health and her conniving, free-spending excesses to make sense of it all. And it is in one single scene, where the Lincoln marriage is shown at its worst, that we get Daniel Day-Lewis, who in the rest of the film is Oscar-good, resorting to the screaming school of overacting that mars his worst work, as for example in *Gangs of New York*.

In short, *Lincoln* is too long, too wordy, too politically indecipherable, and it is hurt rather than helped by the beautiful photographic stills that don't take enough advantage of the cinema as a motion picture art form. The film may be personally inspiring, morally uplifting, historically accurate, and beautifully shot, but as a movie, it's too talky and preachy. Amazingly, Spielberg has managed to make Lincoln the man and *Lincoln* the movie both tiresome and predictable. A missed opportunity.

DEATH, CURIOSITY, AND THE ASCENT OF MAN

Franklin Roosevelt died on April 12, 1945 and on August 6th that same year, his successor, Harry Truman, authorized the dropping of an atomic bomb on Hiroshima, Japan. Three days later a second bomb was exploded over Nagasaki. Together these bombs effectively ended hostilities during World War II—but Franklin Roosevelt never knew who won the war or how it ended.

On April 14, 1865, five days after Robert E. Lee surrendered to Ulysses Grant, thus ending the Civil War, Abraham Lincoln was assassinated—without ever knowing how the post-war peace would work out, what America would look like after the long war that claimed 625,000 American lives, both Blue and Gray.

My father died in 1970 without knowing if I would finish graduate school with the Ph.D. I was working on at the time and that I would finish seven years later.

This goes from the sublime to the ridiculous, but it points out that we are all destined to die without knowing the outcome of something important to us at the time of our death—and that used to trouble me no end.

The more I think of it these days, however, the less it troubles me. And the reason is because the history of mankind is different from and greater than the history of men. Collectively we have come a long way—scientifically, technologically, and artistically—since our first ancestors began walking upright about six million years ago, just yesterday compared to the four and a half billion years the planet has been circling the sun.

During our six-million-year history, we have made spectacular advances that have rightly been described as the Ascent of Man—and yes, thinking metaphorically is one of the advances of our species. In spite of the daily headlines and those who see us as a depraved race of sinners, we should be proud to be human, proud of our species, proud to take our places on the planet for the few years we have.

So what does it matter in the end that we will not know at our deaths exactly how our children's lives will work out or if we've done anything worth the attention of future generations? What does it matter that we will never know what will become of the American Republic? Death is our common destiny. But there is consolation in the knowledge that in our time we have added a little of ourselves to the working out of human history.

Seen from that angle, our lives have meaning, and it is our duty to do something with them, to make our contribution, no matter how small, to the Ascent of Man—even though we are destined to die without knowing how it will all turn out. It is together, collectively, that we as a race of thinking men, *homo sapiens*, make our mark on the universe. It's an uplifting thought, better than heaven.

Storm Tracker: The Ironies of Hurricane Sandy

I've been keeping track of Sandy the Hurricane and the unnamed Nor'easter that have been pounding the mid-Atlantic states with a one-two punch for several hours now. It's a record breaker—by storm surge, rainfall, damage, and duration.

New Jersey, where I was born and raised and where I lived for sixty years, is taking a heavy hit. And I am still worried about my children, their spouses, and my six grandchildren, who all still live there.

Last year they were hit with a hurricane named Irene which knocked out power for days on end and left a huge impression on my children in central and northwest New Jersey. Sandy will be harder on them, at least twice as hard, if the early estimates are even half true.

Irony is retired grandparents moving to hurricane-prone Florida and not having a single one in seven years while normally hurricane-safe New Jersey has now had two. Sometimes it's hard to figure out what God's plan is. Or how the vagaries of weather can figure into the Divine Plan at all. It looks for all the world like there isn't any plan.

In June we did have a semi-hit when hurricane Isaac skirted downtown Tampa and the Republican National Convention, about an hour west of our home in central Florida's Twin Cities, Zephyrhills and Dade City. We seemed pretty vulnerable for a while. But by the time Isaac got to Dade City, he was too tired to do much damage—and anyway, more irony, my wife and I were safely vacationing in New Jersey at the time.

When Sandy caromed off Florida a day or two ago, leaving the East Coast of the state wet and windy, we in Central Florida merely cursed the occasionally brisk breezes we faced on the golf course. "Is that a one or two-club correction?" we asked one another while we mumbled curses under our breath.

Meantime, when all was counted up, New Jersey suffered $30 billion in economic losses, 346,000 homes damaged or destroyed, and 37 people dead. Cleanup costs ran to an estimated $37 billion.

AMERICAN SPORT: DEMOCRATS VS. REPUBLICANS WHY VOTE?

I don't think there's any difference between rooting for a political party and rooting for a sports team. All fans are pretty much alike, so when partisan supporters rant on and on in favor of their candidate and then flip it over to argue against the rival candidate, they behave and sound and look exactly like fans arguing over the Red Sox and Yankees, the Lakers and Celtics, or the Eagles and Redskins. Rooting for political parties and sports teams comes to the same thing—which is to say they are equally unimportant.

Put it this way: trying to understand the political process as we know it, is just as trivial a business as arguing the relative merits of a baseball team; neither one matters very much in the long view. For all the money spent and rhetoric wasted by political parties and candidates during a presidential election year, the end result turns out to be pretty much the same regardless of which candidate is actually elected. And that is because we always get middle-of-the road presidencies that are limited by national and international events, together with advisers who influence the president's thinking and invariably drag left-wing liberal presidents and right wing conservative ones toward the middle of the political spectrum.

And thank God for that. The last thing we need is for extremists of either stripe implementing policy changes that would reshape the country radically. We are fortunate that at the end of the day, it just doesn't matter who the president is. He or she is on a short leash and is not allowed to stray very far from the political center.

And if you still think it matters who the president is, consider this: There were legions of partisan supporters lined up behind Benjamin Harrison when he ran against Grover Cleveland in 1888. And Rutherford Hayes when he ran against Samuel Tilden in 1876. And Calvin Coolidge when he ran against John Davis in 1924. Multitudes once cared very much about those elections, yet today we are hard put to recall who won and who lost. The fact is that it didn't matter then and it doesn't matter now.

And it follows, therefore, that voting doesn't much matter either, especially when the voter can't see the difference between one local councilman and someone from the community running against him (or her). Voters in those cases usually line up as a Democrat or Republican and vote accordingly, but that is maddeningly irresponsible. When you can't see a reason to vote for either candidate, don't vote. That's the only responsible thing to do. And the same reasoning applies to presidential elections.

But, it is argued, one can follow the candidates (at every level) and decide who to vote for on the basis of their positions on the issues. That too is specious because the issues, whatever they happen to be, have to be interpreted and there are always at least two views (interpretations) on every subject (issue). Both views make sense, and the only difference between them is which party a voter happens to be a member of. And even if we can keep an independent mindset and pay attention to what the candidates say and write, we become persuaded by the best orator or the best writer, not necessarily the best ideas.

This obviously makes every vote suspect. If you can't see which candidate is right about the economy, health care, foreign affairs, and so on, how can you cast an intelligent ballot? Once again, the only responsible thing to do is not to vote at all. The worst or best that can happen in any election is that a different person may get to shape the national discourse for a few years before the "minority" party is returned to "power" and thus becomes the "majority" for a few years. And so it goes on and on in a never-ending, meaningless loop. Despite all the self-righteous talk and appeals to high-minded virtue, the political process dwindles down to Super Bowl or World Series smallness. It's all about winning, one season at a time. Nothing more.

If, however, a referendum you oppose or favor is on the ballot, or if one candidate happens to settle on a position that will do you, personally, some good, then by all means cast a vote. Politics always comes down to self-interest. Most of the time, however, elections just don't matter. Enjoy them. Learn to take pleasure in the presidential sweepstakes as high (or low) drama, political theater filled with sex scandals, outright lies, and outrageous smears. What could be more fun?

Addendum. Maureen Dowd, op ed columnist for the *New York Times*, got it almost right in her column ("The Loin King") on Sunday, November 4, two days before the country finally went to the polls to choose between incumbent Barack Obama and Republican challenger Mitt Romney: "Voting for either man seems a shot in the dark. You have to make that vote still confused about who they are, how they've evolved, and where they're leading us." Dowd seems to think it's the responsible thing to do to vote even though it's a "shot in the dark." I'm not so sure it is: if you can't figure out which candidate is best, how can it be in the country's best interest to add your uninformed vote to the general confusion?

SETH AND OSCAR, A MATCH MADE IN HEAVEN

News that Seth MacFarlane has been named host of next year's Oscars has pop culture consumers grinning and strutting because MacFarlane is the creator of a cartoon program on Fox called *Family Guy*. Isn't it cool that one of our own stars has plucked this honor, they seem to be saying and preening at the same time. MacFarlane's honor represents their own entry into acceptable mainstream entertainment and validates their own taste in TV shows. But it ought to alarm them too because it proves they are no longer on the radical cutting edge of contemporary TV; they are now in the cultural mainstream—uncool. Perfectly forgettable.

Maybe MacFarlane's choice is just pathetic, a by-now unnecessary additional proof that we are a nation of adult cartoon watchers, and that this lingering adolescence has intruded into what would normally be our years of maturity. Good grief, is there no point at which we grow up? No point at which we switch from "classic" comic books to the actual classics? No point at which the term "classic rock and roll" becomes an embarrassment? No point at which we replace "pop culture" with real culture?

I suppose not—but it's worth the effort to fight the drift, to raise consciousness, to expand horizons, and to improve taste. Meantime, Mr. MacFarlane will continue giving the people what they want. It's just a shame they don't want more.

THE GOD PARTICLE: GAINS AND LOSSES

Why is the Higgs boson called the God particle? If I have it right, it's because it explains the creation of matter—that is, the existence of all things. God, if the scientists are right, didn't create anything, unless perhaps it was the single spark that exploded the universe into existence, the so-called Big Bang. And even that is getting more doubtful.

Proof of the existence of the Higgs boson has been some fifty years coming and was made possible by the physicists working on the Swiss particle collider at CERN (the European Organization for Nuclear Research) that only weeks ago produced a quantum particle with mass, thus fulfilling the prediction of its existence made by Higgs and other scientists in the 1960s. The Higgs boson. The God particle. The particle that explains all mass and matter. It was an epic discovery, and one that leaves creation myths, including the Garden of Eden, as nothing more than the literary inventions they are, something like the stork story as an explanation for where babies come from.

Science is beautiful in its own right, but it's a shame that it deprives us mere mortals of the comforting fictions we have dreamed up since before recorded history about gods, creation, and life after death. Everything new that we learn about the cosmos and about quantum mechanics is a beautiful testimony to our minds and to the superiority of our species, but how can we not simultaneously feel diminished? How can we not feel deeply the loss of prayer, Bible, God himself?

This is not a new idea, of course, and I am not saying anything here that hasn't been said many times over by better minds than mine, but every individual's discovery of this essential truth is just as painful as the first one. God is hard to give up.

PUNCTUALITY

I saw an ad in an issue of the *Smithsonian* for a wristwatch. I don't wear one any more, not since I started carrying a cell phone (when I remember to). But this two-page ad caught my attention: "We apologize that this watch loses 1 second every 20 million years." The truth is, I've never cared much about the time, and the need for this kind of insane precision is a total mystery to me.

Sometimes someone in a group I'm with will ask the time, and if I happen to be wearing a watch or can pull out my cell phone first, I'll answer the question, "ten to one." Someone else in the group is likely to follow that with, "It's 12:47, to be absolutely precise." "Absolutely precise"? What does it matter as long as it is more or less a quarter to one or ten to one—or twelve forty-seven?

Oh sure, if you set your alarm clock for six AM and it goes off at seven, you might be late for something, but what of it? Most of the appointments in my life do not depend on exact punctuality, and when I *have* to be at a certain place at a certain time, I am. Ninety-nine percent of the time, however, it just doesn't matter all that much. It's impolite to keep people waiting, so I try to be more or less on time, but being a little late (or a little early) doesn't seem to me to be the worst social blunder.

I read once that people from Northern European countries are much more time-conscious than those from Southern European countries, where arriving within an hour of an invitation is considered "on time." I'm okay with that. Relax. You'll get where you're going soon enough.

THE DESIGNATED HITTER: THE BANE OF BASEBALL?

The Colorado Rockies swept their way into the World Series with impressive playoff wins against the Diamondbacks and the Phillies. They finished the season at 90-73, a half game behind the D-backs in their division, but they won 20 of their last 21 games, won a Wild Card playoff spot, and ran like a buzz saw into the World Series against the Boston Red Sox, who had struggled for the last month of the season, had given up a big lead against the Yankees before sealing the deal, and then had fallen behind the Indians three games to one before turning on the afterburners and winning the last three games to win the American League pennant and earn a shot against the red-hot Rockies.

The Sox clobbered the Rockies 13-1 in the first game.

Now anything can happen, and it will be fun to watch these two teams play each other until one has won four of seven, but increasingly the World Series is less a world championship showdown than it is a shadow of what it once was. The country at large still loves to preserve the nostalgic notion that the World Series determines the best team in baseball, but it doesn't, not any more. And the reason, of course, is the presence of a Designated Hitter in the American League, which skews all the won-lost records, all a team's roster decisions, all the balance between offense, defense, speed, and pitching. The AL simply plays a different game from the NL.

I used to live in the New York area and rooted for a long time for the Mets in the National League. Years earlier, before the DH got to the American League in 1973, I rooted for the Casey Stengel Yankees, which won ten AL pennants and seven World Series titles in the twelve years between 1949 and 1960—including five world championships in a row from 1949 to 1953—the last true dynasty in major league baseball. Now, however, I live in the Tampa Bay area and have adopted as my team the Rays, the perennial doormats of the American League East. During this past year, I learned two things that surprised me. First is that it is more fun rooting for the small-market Rays than it ever was rooting for the Big Market Mets or Yankees. And the second, most surprising, thing is that it was fun rooting for a team with a DH.

American League offenses just keep coming at you. There's no relief in sight when you look at their lineups. Soft-hitting pitchers, for example, don't get to the plate in the AL. Because the National League pitchers hit, there is also a greater need for pinch hitters, another dynamic that makes the leagues different. And with pitchers hitting, there is more sacrifice bunting in the NL. The presence of an offensive weapon who never takes the field, also makes AL teams more likely to have good defenses. That is, they don't have to put a poor-fielding player on the field just to get his bat in the lineup. The AL doesn't have to manufacture runs as much as the NL either. And American League managers don't have to pull their starters for a pinch hitter in the middle of a rally. Finally, the famous National League "double switch," designed to get a position player to hit in the lineup before the pitcher is due up, is also unnecessary in the AL.

So the AL plays a more simplified, less strategized game that barely resembles real baseball at all. But it *is* fun to watch. Despite more frequent pitching changes, the games seem quicker, more action dominated, less boring, than NL games. For the first time in my lifelong love of baseball, I can see why the American League, with its DH diminishment, is attractive to fans. I like it too.

But pitting a team with the DH against a team without one, is a travesty. I've known this for years, of course, because the purists have made the point often and loudly over the years. But watching the Red Sox and their offensive juggernaut dismantle the Rockies in Fenway Park in the first game of the World Series brings the entire issue back into focus. It does not even the playing field to use the DH in AL parks and no DH in NL parks. Entire rosters are built on the basis of having your pitcher come to bat four times a game—or having a DH come up four times a game. The Rockies are not worse than the Red Sox, they are just not playing the same game. The only way to ever again make the World Series be a real world championship is to have both leagues play under the same rules.

I never thought I'd say this, but the solution is to bring the DH to the National League. It's really that simple.

Update: The Red Sox swept the Rockies, 4-0.

Democracy, Youth, and Old Age

When I was a young man learning about the work-intensive and time-consuming steps required to enact the simplest piece of legislation, the least contentious of new measures, I grew stridently impatient. It was clearly wrong that good people had to waste endless hours and days and months trying to do something worthwhile. I couldn't wait so long. I was desperate for fast action. I complained bitterly about the mired-down failure of the democratic process. It was depressing at best, spirit-crushing at worst.

Now that I'm an old man, I'm much more patient. Now it seems good to me that change should come slowly, after long and exhaustive debate. After filibusters. After compromises. After presidential vetoes. I don't want professional do-good Liberals putting their permanent imprint on national legislation; nor do I want selfish Conservatives to close the door on scale-balancing social programs. I'm still mostly in favor of left-of-center political agendas, but I don't want the Left making hasty changes—except in the area of human rights. Speedy action often requires further action to correct problems not seen the first time around. You know what they say about haste.

I don't object to change, of course—only quick change. Slow things down, I say. Talk it all over. And then talk some more. Sleep on it. God, it should be pointed out, was remiss when He left out the Eleventh Commandment, Thou shalt not rush. Someone was probably telling him to hurry up, maybe Moses was waiting.

APRIL 28, 2012

Today I am 70 years old.

My father in the 1960s used to talk wistfully about living to see the year 2000, but he came from a line that led short lives, so he knew it was unlikely that he would live to see the new millennium. He was right: he died in 1970 at age 55. When he did the arithmetic back in the 1960s, he knew he'd have to live to age 86 to see 2000. No, he conceded, that was hardly likely. But it pleased him to think that I, his only child, might. After all, I'd only be 58 in 2000. Yes, he smiled, there was a good chance I'd make it.

When I turned 55 in 1997, I wasn't so sure. That was the age when my father and his father had died, both of colon cancer. But in 1969 medical science made a breakthrough in the fight against this particular cancer, which led me to think in 1997 that I might escape the family fate. In the late 1970s, I began having sigmoidoscopies and then a few years later full colonoscopies, procedures that allow doctors to remove colon polyps which otherwise turn slowly into deadly cancers. Modern medicine had extended my life: becoming 58 and actually seeing the year 2000 had become a real possibility. Still, I was surprised and relieved when I finally made it because I hadn't thought, down deep, I'd last that long.

When I turned 60 in 2002, I really did think I had reached old age. No question about it. I was so thrilled that I quit my job, began receiving my pension, and waited impatiently two more years to begin receiving early Social Security benefits. I wanted to experience the retirement part of my life, which I hadn't thought I'd ever see. I was overjoyed that I had cheated death and that I would have a

60-something-year lifespan. My God, that was truly old compared to my poor father and grandfather. And I was grateful. Deeply grateful.

Then I began creeping toward my 70th birthday, one slow year at a time until I was but a year from it—and suddenly I wanted it very badly. I had never even imagined living that long. 70 was really old. In my heart I had known all along that 60 didn't amount to much on the longevity scale, but it was old enough to satisfy my imagination. 70 was different. At 70, no one would ever say "the poor guy died so young." No way. And so I wanted desperately to become 70, to defy the odds that had seemed to argue all my life for an early demise. My tombstone would read 1942-2012, which has a nice, easy-to-compute balance to it. Oh, there may be a little more time left, but it's okay with me. I'm not greedy about longevity. Not anymore.

70 is a wonderful age to be.

TELEOLOGY VS. PELEOLOGY

One chapter of the Believer's Handbook seeks to prove God's existence by examining design in the universe, the study known as "teleology." According to this argument, order implies the existence of God, but this old argument buckles, perhaps collapses, under the weight of modern science's Uncertainty Principle (Werner Heisenberg, 1927), which has shown that order, symmetry, and design are more apparent than real. Much as we all want an orderly universe, one which confirms God's existence and reaffirms our desperate need to believe we are put on earth for a reason, the universe itself seems to be of another mind. So to speak.

Further arguing against a God-implied teleology is the God-denying study of peleology, which posits that no Creator in His right mind would design and build an organism (in his own image) that has to pee out between one and two liters every single day. It's a hopeless mess. Bathrooms have to be everywhere. Surely the Designer could have come up with a urinary tract system better than the one He settled on. So why didn't He?

Of course, the Almighty may have further changes in mind and may decide to implement them at any time. But that brings up another problem. Why would God go back every few eons to alter complicated operating systems (like turning fish fins into arms and legs or swim bladders into lungs)? Why wouldn't He have just gotten it right the first time?

No, an under-attack teleology is not as persuasive as the common sense study of peleology. God's got some explaining to do.

BUMPER STICKER: REAL MEN PRAY

The older I get the more troubled I become over the idea of prayer. Apart from the likelihood that we are merely talking to ourselves, there's the question of why people do it at all. Why does anyone want to have a one-way "conversation" with an all-powerful Creator who apparently has nothing better to do than listen to petitioners? And what on earth does anyone *say*—besides the recital of memorized words? The worst possible excuse for praying is to ask for favors, the supreme gesture of pure selfishness, whether one prays for himself or his friends and relatives—or even large classes and groups of people. And judging from His total indifference to the prayers for it, God clearly doesn't think much about world peace.

About the only reason I can think of to pray is to say thank you. If there's a Creator, He or She will be pleased to hear a thank you once in a while. That much I'm sure of. But so many people have such a litany of suffering—chronic diseases, death of children and parents, no jobs, no education, drug dependencies, the list of horrors never ends—that I often wonder what on earth they could be thanking God for. Sometimes it seems people should be cursing Him for what He's done to them, which makes more sense than thanking Him for their suffering. Maybe real men *don't* pray: If you can't say something nice, don't say anything at all.

DIVIDED I STAND, PART I

I often feel I must be some variation of schizophrenic. Outwardly—in my relationship with the world-at-large—I can't resist being humorous, even bitterly, blackly comical. Droll at best. At worst, the remarks I pass are smart-alecky, snide, and even mean, but I always aim higher, for some combination of wit, sarcasm, and vulgarity (which always amuses me). And I like a straight-faced delivery that often confuses people who aren't completely sure what they heard was a joke. Sometimes they are sure it isn't—and that I'm a total jerk. I'm sorry when a joke or witticism falls flat, but I can't resist them. I just fire away and hope I can bring it off; I do have a lifetime of delivery practice. This drive to see the humorous hidden away in every day events and conversation is hard-wired into my DNA. It's who I am, for better and worse.

Mind you, I am aware that this is not the sort of personality feature anyone should be proud of, and I know that my life would have gone differently, better no doubt, if I could have controlled myself more often, but I've never been able to do much about it. I've tried to root out the nastiness, of course, but my sense of humor, for better or worse, is what it is, and I feel powerless against it, the way a person learns to live with a debilitating physical affliction.

However, I have spent most of my adult life being serious too—mostly as a late bloomer trying to become a better student, and eventually as a scholar who has strung together a long bibliography of serious writing. That man never looks for the cheap joke or the pointed gibe. He is always on message and carefully in control of his words. It hardly seems possible that I can be both these people at the same time. But I am, it seems, that particular variety of schizophrenic.

DIVIDED I STAND, PART II

*You Don't Say. . .*Monday, September 5, 2011

I was born and raised in an Italian ghetto of parents born in New Jersey and Pennsylvania, and of grandparents born in south-central Italy. In my blood there is a hot-headedness that drives me to outbursts that flash for a moment and then go out forever. But I am also an American, the product of a cool-headed, Anglo-influenced school system: my excitability is thus neutralized by patient, even-tempered problem solving. And so it is that, in another sense, I stand divided.

DIVIDED I STAND, PART III

*You Don't Say. . .*Monday, September 5, 2011

I am so thoroughly conditioned by my Puritan work ethic that a friend once observed that I must have descended from John Milton when he lived in Italy. The remark passed as a cleverness because I spent many years studying American Puritanism and because Italians, my friend thought, were incapable of such dedicated, Milton-like study. Putting the defamation in the second part of the equation aside, it is thus, in a related (though perhaps disputed) sense, that I stand divided.

DIVIDED I STAND, PART IV

*You Don't Say. . .*Monday, September 5, 2011

I am a Catholic non-believer, an atheist for all practical purposes, but one who is nonetheless committed to the calming qualities of silent prayer. I can sometimes talk myself into believing in a Creator, but one who has nothing to do with the Bible or with Jesus or with any church or faith. I think of myself as a cultural Catholic (akin to those who comfortably refer to themselves as cultural Jews)—that is, I am one born to the faith but educated to know better. I like the machinery of the Church, the hierarchy, the pomp and ceremony, the smells of incense and candles, the Stations of the Cross, the sacraments, and so on—but I like it all for cultural reasons that tie me to my Italian-American roots, not spiritual ones that I long ago outgrew. And yet I often return to the calming quality of prayers like the silent Hail Mary, even the Act of Contrition. And nothing settles my nerves like the Twenty-third Psalm, "The Lord is my shepherd, / I shall not want," empty words I'm certain, but ones that nonetheless add a quieting benefit to my days. I'm a non-believing man of prayer—once again, a man divided.

SUBSTANCE OVER STYLE?

Or is it the other way around? Everyone always wants to believe that what they have to say counts more than the way they say it. That what they write is more important than their spelling. But the simple and observable truth of the matter is that if a person writes badly, or perhaps just blandly, his writing and his thoughts will be lost forever. No one will be engaged by the ideas if he can't get by the sentences, which is exactly what Oscar Wilde meant when he wrote: "The truth is entirely and absolutely a matter of style."

ETERNAL SILENCE

It's common, after all, for grieving survivors to imagine what their dearly departed would have wanted. "Dad would have wanted me to play in the big game," we hear young athletes say. Sometimes, to go on despite his loss, the grieving survivor dedicates his performance to his or her dead father—or mother or grandparent. Maybe an entire team will wear a black armband, a remembrance and a motivator. It's all very touching. And insincere.

Survivors, after all, have no alternative but to press on, but assuming the dead person would have happily and forgivingly given his blessing about your decision to suck up your grief and go on your camping trip anyway has always seemed bad form to me. I wince when I hear the familiar refrain: "Dad would have wanted me to go." Have the decency to admit that you are acting selfishly, I want to tell them, that your father's death matters less to you than losing a chance to do something you have been looking forward to. And don't forgive yourself by imagining, in the most self-serving sort of way, that your dead dad would have wanted it that way. If he still had feelings, they would be hurt.

The truth of the matter is that at the moment of death, no one has a voice in anything ever again. Survivors can imagine whatever they want the dead person to have thought or said, but the reality is that survivors from that point forward are safe from the reproaches of the dearly departed, who can no longer manage their own finances, state their most deeply felt opinions, defend themselves against enemies and misunderstanding, explain what they really meant, or ask humbly for forgiveness. They have entered their time of eternal silence.

That's why I write.

127

WHAT HAPPENED TO *AVATAR*?

Written March 15, 2010

Sometimes the right thing happens so naturally that no one takes much notice of it. Which is exactly what happened when *Avatar* missed out on all the top honors at the recent Academy Awards, Hollywood's annual pageant of back-slapping self-congratulation.

The movie has already broken all domestic and international box office records with a "grand total" (after a mere three months of 3-D circulation) of more than $2.6 billion, according to the IMDb, the International Movie Database. And director/writer James Cameron has as a result received early pre-canonization that many believe will lead at the earliest possible moment to his becoming Saint James of Tinsel Town.

It has been a giddy ride for Cameron, one that many could see coming as the result of his previous work, which includes such impressive blockbusters as *Titanic* (1997), $1.8 billion worldwide, and the four-movie *Terminator* franchise, $1.4 billion in all. This is a man who has figured out how to make a buck making movies.

So going into Oscar night on March 7, no one would have been surprised by a clean sweep for the gold-plated *Avatar*, which, instead, went down in spectacular, computer-generated flames. The two great prizes of the evening went to *The Hurt Locker*, which captured Best Picture and Best Director honors, the latter going to Kathryn Bigelow, who managed to shoot the movie for the bargain price of $15 million, compared to the estimated $300 to $500 million it took to shoot *Avatar*.

And it was nothing if not sweet justice to give the Best Director award to a woman for the first time in history—a woman who just happened to be the ex-wife of Saint James himself.

It's tempting to think Hollywood voters were rewarding small, independent film makers, like Bigelow, encouraging them to continue following their dreams by working on small gems of cinematic perfection. And *The Hurt Locker* is certainly a good movie, a valuable addition to the growing list of fine independent films that come out more and more often from the American film industry.

But the problem is that it isn't so good as to have unceremoniously dumped *Avatar* from its pre-Oscar sanctification. No, *Avatar* had to contribute to its own demise for *The Hurt Locker* to overtake it on Oscar night.

Which it did. Oscar voters apparently viewed with raised eyebrows this expensive and hugely profitable film as it drifted oddly into a nearly three-hour denunciation of American capitalism. Even Hollywood types, it would seem, have a limit to the hypocrisy they will tolerate.

It may not be too much to hope that voters also saw the silliness of setting this "futuristic" movie in the year 2154 on a distant planet, and then populating it with giant blue people who nonetheless look a lot like Native Americans from the 1800s. They wear loin cloths, shoot with bows and arrows, and worship nature. Is this science fiction—or an American Indian romance? *Avatar* wants to be both but in the end it merely looks lost in its own interplanetary wilderness.

And just maybe the Hollywood types who voted against *Avatar* this year got a little weary of their industry's tiresome, self-righteous, moral outrage, which it wears like a merit badge on all public occasions. There isn't anything wrong of course with a movie like *Avatar* being for conservation, equal rights, and peace; nor is there anything wrong with challenging aspects of American culture that need challenging. But *Avatar* may have struck Oscar voters as insincere, nothing more than a vehicle for spray-shooting clichés that, with neat accompanying 3-D visuals, give the movie a veneer of high morality with a money-grubbing American capitalism at its bleeding heart.

I think Oscar may have gotten it right this time.

LIVING BY SLOGANS

I'm drawn to slogans and bromides that border on tired platitudes, but that also seem to me to be oftentimes elevated to the status of axioms or proverbs. I mean the sort of wisdom you sometimes read on bumper stickers or dig out of fortune cookies. Regardless of what they're called, being fond of them is not, I don't think, something to be proud of.

Most of the ones I like I've borrowed from somewhere else and put into words that work for me, like "Enjoy the process," which is a not-very-clever way to keep myself centered in the moment. The words are pedestrian, of course, and the idea is threadbare, but its directness keeps me in the present, keeps me from getting ahead of myself and worrying about tomorrow's problems today. "Never trouble trouble till trouble troubles you," as my father-in-law used to say.

Reminding myself to enjoy the process is also how I get through parts of a day that are difficult to tolerate, let alone enjoy, like waiting on lines, visiting the dentist, going through airport security. Or just talking to boring people. Take the sweet with the sour, I say—it's all good.

I often have to remind myself to "slow down," mostly because my natural inclination is to speed through everyday activities—hurry to the bank, rush to the Walmart, get a couple of laps in around the park, stop for gas, and be back home in time to clean the gutters before dinner.

Slowing down and enjoying the process were both hard life changes for me, but in the end I discovered (surprisingly) that I liked the slower rhythms of life better than the speedier ones that caused me to race along every road and rush to the front of every line. In fact, inviting someone in a hurry to go ahead of me in the supermarket line makes me feel good—calmer and more in control. And it's a good lesson for the person who eyes me narrowly as he or she edges by with a few groceries in hand.

But saying "Haste makes waste," doesn't suit me—it's one of the platitudes that I can't warm to. It amounts to just another invitation to slow down, after all, and I like the idea very much, but it suits me to say it differently, contradictorily: "Slow is fast," is the way I say it. And slow *is* fast because slowing down usually keeps me from having to do the same job twice, once the wrong way, and then the right way. Haste, you see, really does makes waste.

A few years back, everyone was talking about "multi-tasking," but that sort of speed-up keeps me from enjoying anything I ever do. I'd rather slow down and uni-task. I want to be disciplined and deliberate, not fast. Slow down and calm down, I say. Keep your composure. Don't worry, don't hurry. That's the ticket.

The same idea applies to what passes for conversation these days. Words fly around so fast that there isn't room any more for even the shortest of thoughtful pauses. I have to remind myself that I don't have to say anything in response to sweaty, over-heated words when they're hurled at me, words that are self-centered and self-congratulatory and aren't really being spoken to me at all. I do have the right, as they say on television cop shows, to remain silent. And I do.

When I feel my life speeding up, however, as it wants to do when left to its own devices, I sometimes have to tell myself to "dial it down," or "take it down a notch," two hopeless but useful slogans for calming myself and simplifying my life. John Wooden, the legendary basketball coach at UCLA, used to say, "Be quick, but don't hurry."

Wooden had another slogan that I like enormously: "Make every day a masterpiece," he used to say. That one's so good, I can't believe it came from a basketball coach, and not, say, from Leonardo DaVinci or Pablo Picasso. Or maybe Dr. Phil.

I think Wooden also said "there is no I in team," but that one's just annoying.

SHORT SHOTS

CAUSE OF DEATH

All "cause of death" information seems vaguely interesting in a statistical sense. That is, by compiling all the data, we learn something about the things that snuff out lives on this planet—and that's good. The phrase takes on a vastly different color, however, when we hear from a doctor what is likely to be our own cause of death.

SUCCESS

On occasion, everyone becomes vulnerable to the temptations of management and/or politics. The impulse should be fought off.

VIRTUE

The only middle-class virtue more highly over-rated than good table manners is punctuality.

The Single Most Over-Rated Novel in American Literary History

It's *The Great Gatsby*, the celebrated 1925 novel by F. Scott Fitzgerald. It's the story of Jay Gatsby's compulsion to reconstruct an adolescent crush that didn't work out for him. This is not praiseworthy behavior. It's delusional—and typical of the almost-always empty-headed Fitzgerald. As Edmund Wilson put it in *The Shores of Light* (1952): "Fitzgerald has been given a gift for expression without very many ideas to express."

Looking Foolish

It's pathetic these days to see so many big-bellied, sixty-five-year-old men, some balding, some with gray pony tails, leaning on their motorcycles and wearing faded Bruce Springsteen tee shirts.

Rock and Roll

Rock music is a tonic for the adolescent soul and an embarrassment to the adult.

COROLLARY

The only rock music an adult can bear is the music of his own adolescence—and what he is after is the past, not music appreciation.

HAPPINESS

Happiness should be the byproduct of a well-spent life, not the goal.

Printed in the United States
By Bookmasters